T. S. ELIOT'S
MAJOR POEMS & PLAYS

including
Introduction
Biography
Commentary on Major Poems and Plays
Commentary on Modern Poetry and Drama
Selected Bibliography
Selected Examination Questions

NOTES

by
Robert B. Kaplan, Ph.D.
University of Southern California

consulting editor
James L. Roberts, Ph.D.
Department of English
University of Nebraska

D1721681

Cliff's Notes
INCORPORATED
LINCOLN, NEBRASKA   68501

'ISBN   8220-1246-4

CONTENTS

INTRODUCTION.. 5
BIOGRAPHY... 7
SELECTED BIBLIOGRAPHY.. 8
MODERN POETRY 9
ELIOT'S THEORY OF POETRY......................................15
THE POEMS

    THE LOVE SONG OF J. ALFRED PRUFROCK...........17
        Section I   (Lines 1-74)..................................20
        Section II (Lines 75-110)..............................22
        Section III (Lines 111-131)..............................22
    THE WASTE LAND...24
        Section I   The Burial Of The Dead..............31
        Section II A Game Of Chess......................35
        Section III The Fire Sermon.........................37
        Section IV Death By Water...........................43
        Section V What The Thunder Said 44
    THE HOLLOW MEN..51
    JOURNEY OF THE MAGI......................................52
    GERONTION..54
    ASH WEDNESDAY 56
    THE FOUR QUARTETS..58
INTRODUCTION TO DRAMA...61

THE PLAYS

    MURDER IN THE CATHEDRAL.............................64
    THE FAMILY REUNION.......................................72
    THE COCKTAIL PARTY.......................................74
    THE CONFIDENTIAL CLERK...............................76

A GENERAL EVALUATION..78
QUESTIONS.. 79

INTRODUCTION

No single person has influenced the development of modern American poetry quite as much as T. S. Eliot, both as poet and as critic. His first serious publication appeared in 1915; Henry James (1843-1916) was still alive; indeed, Emerson and Longfellow had died only some thirty years earlier, and Whitman, Whittier, and Holmes only some twenty years earlier. Eliot is roughly contemporary with the generation of Edwin Arlington Robinson, Robert Frost, Carl Sandburg, Vachel Lindsay, Willa Cather, H. L. Mencken, Sinclair Lewis, and Robinson Jeffers, while men like Fitzgerald, Faulkner, Hemingway, e. e. cummings, Dos Passos, and Thurber are a decade younger. Eliot's contribution is startling not only in its inherent importance, but in its coming so early in the twentieth century, for Eliot's poetry was as different from anything in the nineteenth century as it was different from anything in the fifteenth. He derived his influences from Byron, Bergson, Babbitt, and the French Symbolist poets. These influences, along with an essentially pessimistic view of the plight of modern man, he combined into a poetry and a critical philosophy which has to a large extent shaped the directions of modern poetry in America and to a certain extent in England as well. Whether his influence is salutary is a question still impossible to answer. Certainly the half century since his first publication has given rise to other poets who might have provided the leadership in American poetry: William Carlos Williams, Wallace Stevens, Robert Frost, to name a few. But the fact remains that it was Eliot and his school — essentially the imagist school, including Ezra Pound and Amy Lowell — who have shaped the course of literary development. Before any detailed discussion of Eliot's poetry can be undertaken, it is first necessary to understand why his influence has been as pervasive as it has.

Eliot has, in many of his poems, portrayed as hero that man who feels a sense of his own inadequacy and impotence, and who is painfully aware of the banality and futility of his own life as well as of life in general. This anti-hero struggles against his situation, but he is predestined to fail, partially as a result of what he is, partially as a result of inadequate striving — a further sign of his inherent inadequacy. His character derives from the common Adam's curse explicit in Calvinism. This sense of failure, Eliot has expressed in a psychological symbolism in turn derived from Freud and to a certain extent from Jung. Poetically, he mixes the techniques of "free verse" with snatches of extremely colloquial conversation, echoing his sense of kinship with the unlettered masses, and with juxtapositions of past and present time, reflecting both his philosophical concern with the concept of time and his belief in the *past* as significant in terms of meaningful ritual and tradition. It is this latter conviction which quite probably led him to abandon "young" America for the older civilization of England and the older ritual of the Church of England. In the introduction to *For Lancelot Andrews,* he describes himself as "an Anglo-Catholic in religion, a classicist in literature, and a royalist in politics." This self-analysis is probably as accurate as any more complex scholarly statement.

Such a brief and generalized statement can in no way be considered a valid summary of the carefully evolved and sincerely held philosophical position of a lifetime for a man of Eliot's intellectual accomplishments, yet it may provide enough of a generalization to make Eliot's literary position intelligible. As the more important of his poems are discussed in the subsequent sections of this set of notes, more specific attention will be paid to the particular application of various of the general ideas expressed above. Suffice it to say for the moment, Eliot is not an easy poet to read. He is difficult because he consciously made his poetry difficult. An intelligent reading of his work requires a knowledge of Jung, of Sir James Fraser, of the legends surrounding the Holy Grail, of the philosophy of Bergson, of Dante and medieval French and Italian literature, of classical literature, and of the literature of English Renaissance, to name just a few of his sources.

Such a set of notes as this one cannot do much more than serve to open up the obscurity of the poetry. But the student must read the poetry. These notes can talk only about the parapharasable content of the poetry; they cannot really talk about the poetry. Such a statement would be true of literature in general, but it is particularly true for poetry, for poetry is an oral form, written to be read aloud, and its effects depend only partly upon *what* it says. Most of its meaning derives from how what is said is said. Form and meter, metaphor and image, can be talked about as one can speak of the physical principles of flying buttresses or suspension bridges, but no amount of description can replace the poem, as no amount of architectural terminology can replace the cathedral of Notre Dame or the George Washington bridge. Poetry is the highest expression of the development of any language; a prose explanation of a poem is to the poem as a prose explanation of a joke is to the joke. Having read these notes without the poetry, the student will have at his command a knowledge of a certain number of facts about Eliot's poetry; but until he has read the poetry itself, he will not know that poetry. In short, these notes are intended as a supplement to the poems, not as a substitute for them. Such notes are designed to help a student understand what he reads in the same way that a set of lectures are intended as a help, but never to become his exclusive reading, nor to replace or abridge the essential reading itself.

BIOGRAPHY

T[homas] S[tearns] Eliot was born in St. Louis, Missouri, in 1888 of a transplanted New England family of Unitarian faith and puritan inclination. His ancestors include such a distinguished person as C. W. Eliot, one time president of Harvard, as well as a number of educators, writers, and ministers whose names are prominent in the history of American letters. He studied at the Smith Academy in St. Louis, and published his first poetry in the *Smith Academy Record* in 1905. His early reading included notably the *Rubaiyat of Omar Khayyam,* and the poetry of D. G. Rossetti and Byron. The Byronic influence remained with him for twenty years. He received an undergraduate degree from Harvard University where he had concentrated his attention on philosophy and logic. He had come under the influence of the critic Irving Babbitt, and Santayana. Having completed his undergraduate work in three years, he went to Paris, to the Sorbonne, during 1910-11, where he was tutored by Alain-Fournier and where he heard lectures by Bergson. During the years from 1907 to 1910, while he was at Harvard as an undergraduate, he contributed some poems, including the Harvard Class Ode for 1910, to the *Harvard Advocate.* In the Fall of 1911 he returned to Harvard to attempt graduate study, and he began to investigate the philosophy of F. H. Bradley under the direction of Josiah Royce. He also tried to study Sanskrit. He became an Assistant in Philosophy, and in the Spring of 1914 met Bertrand Russell. In the Summer of 1914, he spent some weeks on a fellowship at Marburg in Germany, and in the fall of that year he entered Merton College, Oxford, where he finished his formal studies. On June 26, 1915 he married Miss Vivienne Haigh Haigh-Wood, daughter of the painter Charles Haigh Haigh-Wood, and took up residence in London. He tried teaching, first at the High Wycombe Grammar School, and later at the Highgate School, but he gave it up after a year or two, and found a position in Lloyds Bank where he remained until 1925. During this period, he supplemented his income by lecturing, book-reviewing and editorial work (he edited the *Criterion* from 1922-1939). In 1916, approximately, he finished his doctoral dissertation, entitled "Experience and the Objects of Knowledge, in the Philosophy of F. H. Bradley." Since he did not return to the United States for almost twenty years, however, he did not receive his degree. His first important poem, *The Love Song of J. Alfred Prufrock,* appeared in *Poetry* in 1915. (See discussion p. 20. For a selected bibliography of his important publications see p. 8). In 1925, Eliot joined joined the publishing firm of Faber and Gwyer, later Faber and Faber. In 1927, he was confirmed into the Church of England, and in the same year he renounced his American citizenship and became a British subject.

He gave the Clark Lectures at Trinity College, Cambridge in 1926 and he lectured at Harvard in 1932, at the University of Virginia in 1933 and at the University of Chicago in 1950. He received the Order of Merit and the Nobel Prize in Literature both in 1948. Mrs. Eliot, from whom he separated in 1933, died early in 1947, and ten years later, in 1957, Eliot married Valerie Fletcher, his secretary. He died on January 4, 1965, in London.

SELECTED BIBLIOGRAPHY

Prufrock and Other Observations, 1917.

Poems, 1920. [including "Gerontion," "Burbank with a Baedeker...," "Sweeney Erect," "The Hippopotamus," "Dans le Restaurant," "Mr. Eliot's Sunday Morning Service," "Sweeney Among the Nightingales," and other poems.]

The Sacred Wood, 1920. (essays)

The Waste Land, 1922.

The Hollow Men, 1925.

For Lancelot Andrews, 1928. (essays)

Ash Wednesday, 1930.

Selected Essays: 1917-1932, 1932 (essays)

The Use of Poetry and the Use of Criticism, 1933. (essays)

After Strange Gods, 1934. (essays)

Elizabethan Essays, 1934. (essays)

The Rock, 1934. (drama)

Murder in the Cathedral, 1935 — film version 1951. (drama)

Essays Ancient and Modern, 1936. (essays)

The Family Reunion, 1939. (drama)

The Idea of a Christian Society, 1939. (essays)

The Music of Poetry, 1942, (essays)

The Four Quartets, 1943.

The Cocktail Party, 1949. (drama)

The Confidential Clerk, 1953. (drama)

The Complete Poems and Plays of T. S. Eliot: 1909-1950, 1952 [including the various fragments, the "Ariel Poems," the minor poems, and the *Old Possum's Book of Practical Cats.*]

MODERN POETRY

In the century since the first publication of Walt Whitman's *Leaves of Grass* (1855), the art of writing poetry has undergone several revolutions. In the period between 1930 and 1955, roughly, Anglo-American poetry has produced a crop of poet-critics who are particularly conscious of their art and their techniques. This consciousness stems to a large extent from the influence of Eliot.

In general, modern literature, and particularly modern poetry, is the heir of many schools and many traditions. It is not a thing in isolation, sprung whole out of the modern age. However, it is generally agreed that the modern idiom of poetry depends primarily on two traditions — the metaphysical, stemming from John Donne (1571[?]-1631), and the symbolist, stemming from Etienne Stéphane Mallarmé (1842-1898). The metaphysical poets pursued integrity by analysis; the symbolist poets invoked it by intuition and suggestion. The symbolists tried to hasten the disintegration of the modern world by a derangement of the senses in order that by recombining the exploded elements with little or no relations to their former structures, they might construct a truer world of inner reality. Since grammar, syntax, and structure are also logical entities related to semantics, the symbolists discarded or exaggerated traditional usage. The metaphysical poets, on the other hand, used all their intellectual as well as their intuitive and suggestive resources to bring congruity to discordant ideas and images.

Although categories are never really satisfactory, these two categories, the metaphysical and the symbolist, constitute convenient tags or labels, or handles with which to get hold of some essential distinctions. The metaphysical poets are generally thought to be Eliot, Pound, Amy Lowell, and a number of others. The symbolist group includes writers like Wallace Stevens, William Carlos Williams, Theodore Roethke, Dylan Thomas, and others. The metaphysical school is characterized by its intellectual complexity, its wasteland derogation of possibilities, and its lack of physical joy. It lacks the qualities of song, of incantation, of passion which characterize English poetry in general. Rather it has connotations of harshness, obscurity, and dogma, and it is colored by intellectual pride and wry despair. It is further characterized by metrical experimentation of a particular kind. The metrical experimentation tries to achieve a relationship in which the metrical structure can become a key metaphor within the larger metaphor of the poem as a whole, which in turn deals with problems in reality.

More immediately than from John Donne, the contemporary influence has been derived from the so-called imagist school of poets, which held the literary stage, at least in the United States, roughly from 1909 to 1917. Probably the most important and informative summary of the imagist position was provided in the "credo" of the group, published in *Some Imagist Poets,* in 1915. The credo included the use of language of common speech, precision, the creation of new rhythms, absolute freedom in choice of subject matter, the evocation of images in hard, clear poetry, and concentration. In general, this credo has its origins in the literary philosophy of the British critic, T. E. Hulme. The insistence on the language of common speech is based largely on Hulme's distinctions between classic and romantic poetry. Hulme wrote that accurate description is a perfectly legitimate object of poetry. He stressed accuracy, precision, and definiteness, and objected strenuously to what he called "damp" verse. He felt that poetry should be illuminated by the light of ordinary day, not by a light "that never was on land or sea."

The experimentation with verse forms was in a sense also a rebellion against nineteenth century romanticism. William Wordsworth (1770-1850) had rejected the artificial language of the neo-classic poetic convention of the 18th century. He had been corrected in his complete rejection by Samuel Taylor Coleridge (1772-1834). But both of these writers, while rejecting the language had, rather inconsistently, accepted the metrical conventions. While they both preferred the simpler metrical forms, they were both bound by the existing metrical conventions. These conventions insist on the accurate measuring of metrical feet into iambic, trochaic, anapestic, or dactylic meters, and on a relatively regular number of such measures per line of verse. The convention ignores the value of the relative duration of pause, and accepts traditional stanzaic forms.

NOTE: This stanza is in the traditional ballad form, rhyming abcb. The meter is iambic [x /], and the lines alternate tetrameter in lines one and three with trimeter in lines two and four. Notice the necessary false stress on the word *sailor* in line three which results from strict attention to metrical pattern:

Sir Patrick Spens [ballad]

x / x / x / x /
O up and spake an elder knight,

x / x / x /
Sat at the king's right knee

x / x / x / x /
"Sir Patrick Spens is the best sailor,

x / x / x /
That ever sailed the sea."

NOTE: These lines constitute a couplet, rhyming aa. The meter is trochaic [/ x], and both lines are tetrameter lines. As in the previous illustration, notice the absolute regularity of the meter.

/ x / x / x / x
Double, double, toil and trouble;

/ x / x / x / x
Fire burn, and cauldron bubble.

[from *Macbeth,* Act IV, sc. i]

NOTE: This is again a four line stanza, but not a ballad stanza. Here each line is anapestic [x x /], and each line contains four such feet, making the pattern tetrameter. Again, the meter is extremely regular, and the regularity tends to produce a "galloping" meter. The rhyme scheme in this stanza is aabb. This meter is less commonly used in English than either of the first two, since it is not native to English and since it does produce the galloping effect. The native rhythm of English is basically iambic, but that does not mean that it is constantly or exclusively iambic. It does mean that iambic meter and particularly iambic pentameter is most commonly used.

The Destruction of Sennacherib

```
x   x  / x  x    /   x   x / x   x /
```
The Assyrian came down like the wolf on the fold,

```
x    x  / x    x    /  x  x  / x x   /
```
And his cohorts were gleaming in purple and gold;

```
x    x   /  x  x   /   x  x   /  x   x /
```
And the sheen of their spears was like stars on the sea,

```
 x   x  /  x   x   /  x x   /    x x/
```
When the blue wave rolls nightly on deep Galilee

George Gordon Lord Byron

NOTE: This is not a complete stanza, but only part of one. The lines are very long. The meter of this passage is dactylic, although there are some substitutions of other feet in the last three lines. There are, however, six stressed syllables in every line; therefore, the meter is hexameter. Again, this is not a very common meter in English. Notice that these lines do not rhyme.

Evangeline

```
/ x   x / x   x / x    x  /  x x   /   x    x
```
This is the forest primeval. The murmuring pines and the

```
/ x .
```
hemlocks,

```
/  x   x  /  x  x / x    /  x x /  x
```
Bearded with moss, and in garments green, indistinct in

```
x  /  x
```
the twilight,

```
/   x   / x x /   x  / x / x    x / x
```
Stand like Druids of eld, with voices sad and prophetic,

```
/  x  / x /   x  /  x / x   x
```
Stand like harpers hoar, with beards that rest on their

```
/ x
```
bosoms.

Henry Wadsworth Longfellow

Other types of feet are possible. These are the spondee [/ /], the pyrrhic [x x], and the amphibrach [x / x], but these are substitution feet, and it would be most unlikely to find whole lines made of any of these, let alone whole stanzas. Certain common stanza forms also constitute a part of the convention. The most commonly employed stanza forms are:

The *couplet:* These lines are commonly pairs of lines with exact aa, bb, cc rhyme schemes. The metrical patterns may vary, but if they are iambic pentameter, then the couplet is called "heroic." That form was extremely common in the 18th century.

The *ballad:* This is a four line stanza, alternating tetrameter and trimeter lines having a rhyme scheme abcd, or sometimes abab. The *quatrain* is a variation of this form, but its lines may be of any length or metrical pattern, and its rhyme scheme may be abba or aabb.

Rhyme Royal: A seven line stanza of iambic pentameter with the rhyme scheme ababbcc. It is also called the *Chaucerian stanza.*

Octava Rima: An eight line iambic pentameter stanza with the rhyme scheme abababcc. It was used effectively by Byron in his *Don Jaun,* and is therefore sometimes called the *Don Juan Stanza.*

Terza Rima: An interlocking series of three line stanzas having the rhyme scheme aba bcb cdc, etc. It was used by Dante in the *Divine Comedy.*

Spenserian Stanza: A nine line stanza in which the first eight lines are iambic pentameter and the ninth line is iambic hexameter. The rhyme scheme is ababbcbcc.

Sonnet: A fourteen line stanza of iambic pentameter. There are really two different forms of this stanza; the *Italian or Petrarchan* form divides into an octave rhyming abbaabba and a sestet rhyming cdecde or cdcdcd, and the *Shakespearean* or *Elizabethan* form divides into three quatrains and a couplet, commonly rhyming abab cdcd efef gg. Other rhyme schemes are also possible.

Blank Verse: Not exactly a stanza form, but rather a series of lines of unrhymed iambic pentameter.

A number of French forms were also introduced into English literature. The more common of these are the *ballade,* the *rondeau,* the *rondel,* the *triolet,* and the *villanelle.* The *ode* also occurs with relative frequency, but the form of the ode has come to be very loosely interpreted.

The modern poets have rebelled against these metrical conventions as they did against artificiality in diction and language. In the matter of langauge, they had the mistakes of Wordsworth and the corrections of Coleridge to serve as guides, so that extremes did not develop again until fairly recently. The experimentation in metrics, however, quickly became chaotic and highly diversified. This experimentation is usually included under the term "free verse" or its French equivalent *"vers libre."* Obviously, since the experimentation was diversified, "free verse" is not one form, but in reality includes all the forms which cannot be classified in the limits of the convention. The Imagist poets completed the revolution begun by Wordsworth. They emancipated diction, meter, and rhythm from formal artificiality, and they showed the poet that he was free not only to create, but to make for himself the laws under which he would create. Eliot was one of those who made his own laws and who experimented widely with verse forms, even creating a metrical device which permits him to play with language for comic effects.

Simply as a matter of contrast, the other school of poets, the symbolist group, has in it elements of joy and wonder in the natural world. It celebrates the body as well as the soul, both in a unified duality combining within itself emotion and intellect, good and evil. It is often incantatory and passionate. It is affirmative in its sense of life. To a certain extent this group derives from Mallarmé, whose poetry Paul Valéry described as primitive and incantatory, but it also derives, in part at least, from a more immediate American source; from Walt Whitman. And, it has similar roots in England in the work of Gerard Manley Hopkins.

In very general terms, the preceding paragraphs attempt to provide a background for the changes taking place in contemporary poetry, and attempt to indicate what contemporary poetry is. It is impossible, of course, to limit background. Each of the contemporary poets mentioned stands at the end of a long tradition of English poetry. The forerunners of contemporary poets are also not isolated in history. All are part of a much longer tradition. To make a careful analysis of the tradition, one would have to return to *Beowulf* and to examine the great bulk of material which constitutes the Anglo-American tradition since then. Obviously such an investigation is simply not practicable here. But one can identify proximal causes. Whitman and the Imagists are proximal causes. There are two dominant tendencies which wed the divergent streams of contemporary poetry; the attempt to use the language of common speech, and the insistence on metrical experimentation. These tendencies derive from different sources and from different motivations in the two dominant schools, but they function universally in contemporary poetry regardless of school or origin. Both groups of poets who form the general foundation of modern poetry are interested in establishing an oral poetry closely allied to common speech, in rhythm, and in language.

ELIOT'S THEORY OF POETRY

As early as 1933, in *The Use of Poetry and the Use of Criticism,* Eliot remarked that he considered the theater to be the ideal medium for poetry. In 1936, after the moderate success of *Muder in the Cathedral,* he generalized further by saying, in a radio talk, that he believed poetry to be "the natural and complete medium for drama." That talk revealed that Eliot considered poetry preferable to prose in drama because it provided, under the action, the advantage of reinforcement and intensification of feeling and excitement through the "musical pattern" of verse. In more recent years Eliot has returned strongly to that argument. At times in his handling of verse in the plays, as well as in certain of his poems, Eliot has recreated the incantatory rhythms of liturgy. In general, however, his verse has modern vocabulary and cadence.

In "The Rock" (1934) Eliot mixed seven or eight different types of verse, ranging from the Kiplingesque comic song through an imitation of the clumsy unmusical free verse (which Eliot disliked) in the lines ascribed to the Redshirts; from the heavy, regular, footstamping beat of the lines belonging to the Blackshirts, to the lines of the final chorus, which have a Swinburnean quality. In general, the standard measure is iambic pentameter but this gives way repeatedly in passages of excitement to a kind of poetic prose of highly irregular stress (sometimes involving anapestic substitution).

In *Murder in the Cathedral,* the verse is not so miscellaneous as in "The Rock": therefore, the feeling of structural orderliness is greater. In "Poetry and Drama" (1950), Eliot explained that in his search for a neutral style, neither too modern nor in the wrong way archaic, he had worked toward the effect achieved in *Everyman,* a popular morality play of the 15th century. In fact, in the rhyming passages of the Tempters' dialogues with Becket, one can see the irregularly assorted stresses, four, to a line, which closely imitate the meter of the older play. Eliot even introduced alliteration to bring his line closer to his model. In other words, Eliot depended heavily, in this play, upon models drawn from Old and Middle English alliterative verse, which is a verse form based not upon syllable counting, but upon a poetic line containing four stresses falling upon syllables which have the same initial sound. The line is often broken into two parts by a split, or caesura, between the first two and the last two stresses. The lines are often run-on rather than end-stopped; that is, the end of the idea does not coincide with the end of a verse line, but is carried over to the next line. The following example translated from *Beowulf* may serve to illustrate the points:

/   /   /   /
Over *b*reaking *b*illows,   with *b*ellying sail

/   /   /   /
And *f*oaming *b*eak,   like a *f*lying *b*ird

/   /   /   /
The *s*hip *s*ped,   until next day's *s*un

/   /   /   /
*Sh*owed *s*ea-cliffs,   *sh*ining high *h*ills

/   /
And *s*preading *h*eadlands . . .

Speaking again in "Poetry and Drama," Eliot describes his line as being of varying length and as having varying numbers of syllables, but as being characterized by three stresses in each line. These stresses are not syllabic stresses, but only the most dominant stresses in a line, disregarding all minor degrees of stress. He states, too, that the line is marked by a caesura. This principle, along with the four-stress alliterative rhythm mentioned above, constitutes the verse pattern of *The Family Reunion* and *The Cocktail Party.* In general the verse in these two later plays is more artificial and less intense than in the earlier plays, and Eliot acknowledged this fact himself.

More or less simultaneously with the developments in his dramatic verse methods, Eliot produced a series of poems called *Landscapes* (1934). These poems indicate Eliot's readiness for certain musical experiments in the following *Four Quartets.* As early as "Portrait of a Lady" (1910), he had experimented with the music of speech cadences. "Music," in the *Four Quartets,* goes beyond denoting speech alone; it implies the sound and rhythm of spoken words, but it also signifies the structure of interrelations among different kinds of speech and other poetic materials. The music extends from the colloquial to the oratorical. It was Eliot's contention that, after poetic idiom has been stabilized by a return to speech, the time is ripe for musical elaboration to begin.

In general, then, up to the period between *The Waste Land* and *The Hollow Men* (1921-1925), Eliot's verse could be scanned in the same manner that most verse in English can be scanned. In later poetry this is not so. This new form marks a break with the tradition of English non-lyrical verse. Up to this time, Eliot was trying to put new content into old forms, and to revive the forms by returning to older methods. But by 1942, when he wrote *The Music of Poetry,* nearly ten years after *The Use of Poetry and the Use of Criticism,* and after the experiences of "The Rock," *Murder in the Cathedral,* and *The Family Reunion,* he was able to say that he believed that every language dictated its own speech rhythms, laws, restrictions, and license. He pointed out that any living language is always changing, and that a poet must make the best of the change.

Eliot's experiments in the writing of dramatic verse led him to the creation of the meter he has employed for non-dramatic purposes in the *Four Quartets,* which is certainly the mature achievement of a poet who has long experimented with the English language. His new verse forms have undoubtedly had a significant effect on his contemporaries and on his followers.

Thus Eliot, operating simultaneously as poet and critic, experimented with verse and language and reported the results of his experimentations as his critical opinion.

There are basic philosophical ideas which also play a part in the development of Eliot's verse, but these will be taken up in connection with the major poems and plays individually rather than introduced here.

THE LOVE SONG OF J. ALFRED PRUFROCK

Eliot was a peculiar poet in a sense. His production is relatively meager in bulk. Compared with a poet like Masefield or Kipling or Browning or

Tennyson, his total quantity of production is very small indeed, yet his influence is far greater than any of them. Not only is his quantity limited, but the variety of his work is also somewhat limited; that is, he was not concerned with a great variety of ideas, but he explored thoroughly those ideas with which he was concerned. Prufrock is the earliest statement of a number of themes that Eliot was to explore again and again in his subsequent poetry. That is not to say that his position never altered; quite the contrary, his view of these problems did change over the years, but the problems with which he concerned himself did not change.

The Love Song of J. Alfred Prufrock is the song of a being divided between passion and timidity. It is a song of frustration and emotional conflict. On the paraphrasable level, the poem starts off with action, an invitation to go, and moves to inaction and a desire for inactivity to the point of enforced release from pain. The poem is a monologue, spoken by "I" who is presumably Prufrock. He talks to a "you" who appears to be a companion, perhaps a woman. The world in which these events occur is a world in which action is trivial. In many ways, the world of this poem resembles the world of Alexander Pope's "Rape of the Lock," a world of "polite society" in which a tea party is a significant event and a game of cards is the only way to stave off boredom. Ennui extends even into the relation between the sexes. The literal situation of the poem suggests turn-of-the-century Boston with its manners, its poses, its summer houses at Hyannis Port, its literary teas, and its Ivy League graduates. The emotional situation of the poem builds from the first faint suggestion of strain in the opening lines, to an incredible tension, to a relaxation of tension, to a cessation of all action. The verse is essentially iambic, and the general pattern of the poem is dominated by couplets. For example, the first eleven lines have the rhyme scheme aabccddeeff. The length of the lines varies considerably. For example, the first line is a four-stress line while the second line is a six-stress line. Some lines extend to seven or more stresses, while a few contain as few as three stresses.

The form of the monologue is perhaps borrowed from Browning, while the plot of the poem may be derived from Henry James' "Crapy Cornelia," a story published in 1909 in which a middle-aged bachelor named White-Mason visits a younger widow named Cornelia Worthington in order to propose marriage but reconsiders because of the differences in their ages and their worlds. Beyond these more apparent debts, the poem employs the self-irony of Laforgue, but adapted to a serious purpose. Like much of Eliot's other work, individual lines or phrases are borrowed from other works and function to recall those works. For example, the image "squeeze the universe into a ball" is borrowed from Andrew Marvell's "To His Coy Mistress." In the original, however, the line has sexual value. The epigraph is from Dante's *Inferno*. There are also obvious references to *Hamlet*. This technique of borrowing lines and putting them into a new context becomes more important in Eliot's later poetry.

Prufrock is an interesting tragic figure. He is a man caught in a sense of defeated idealism and tortured by unsatisfied desire. He is unimportant to others, but aware of his own despair. He does not dare to seek love because he is afraid of disappointment, partially because he is afraid that he could not find love to begin with, and partially because even if he could find it, it would not satisfy his needs. For Eliot, Prufrock's position is an image of the sensitive man caught in a stupid world. Prufrock is an aging romantic entrapped by a rotting world of pseudo-gentility. While he is aware of beauty, he is too inhibited to seek it, too hesitant to reach for it, and too surrounded by the sordid to achieve it. To add to his problems, Prufrock also has a tragic flaw. As a result of his timidity he has become incapable of action of any sort. These problems coupled with his tragic flaw unite to destroy him. His values derive from the traditions of romantic love — witness the "sea-girls" — and he is consciously unheroic — witness his own comparison of himself with Hamlet. These factors should combine to make him a comic figure, but his added awareness makes him a tragic rather than a comic figure because he reminds one that no problem is trivial to the man who has it.

The action of the poem is limited; that is, the poem contains little overt action, but rather the action consists of the interplay of impressions in the mind. Literally, the "I" and "you" of the poem are not two persons but rather two aspects of the same person — the public personality and the ego. In addition to contributing to the effect of monologue, the use of the pronouns creates the impression of a man talking to himself in the mirror. The ego goes along with the physical body; it is interpreted through the physical body. Prufrock's physical body is thin, wispy, weak. The physical body is judged by others and condemned. And the ego is injured by the disgrace of the personality. The two, opposed to each other and united to each other, destroy Prufrock, and at the end of the poem "we" drown.

The epigraph heightens Prufrock's frustration. It refers to the torture of Guido da Montefeltro in the eighth circle of the *Inferno*. He is tortured in hell for the sin of fraud through evil council. Prufrock is unlike him in the sense that he does not intentionally participate in evil, but he is like him in that he is guilty of fraud because he has perverted the human reason (his own) by directing it into pointless fantasy. Even the dissimilarity between the two figures serves to heighten the irony of Prufrock's situation by pointing up Prufrock's lack of heroic characteristics while it indicates that he too is in a kind of hell. Prufrock lives in a world of fantasy and daydreams of which the monologue itself is a symptom. In this unreal world, he has allowed his ideal conceptions (of women, for example, as indicated by the sea-girls) overshadow his real life. Thus he has neither accepted nor rejected love. Rather he has created a false notion of it which has prevented him from taking any kind of action. Through the course of the poem, he has grown out of sentimentality, but he has found nothing to replace it. And his tragedy is simply that he is a man driven by desire for something that he cannot achieve. Thus, while he cannot abandon the illusions of his fantasy world, he cannot accept the realities of the other world in which the women talk, quite probably foolishly, of Michelangelo.

Prufrock's name itself is interesting in terms of the poem. The name Prufrock is a real one which Eliot borrowed from a St. Louis family, but in spite of its reality, it is rather precious. The obtrusive initial at the beginning recalls both Lincoln's and Mark Twain's distrust of men who "part their names in the middle." "Alfred" suggests perhaps a certain refinement accompanied by a certain reserve. All these combine to indicate the character of Prufrock so successfully that *prufrockian* has entered the language as an adjective suggesting a kind of archaic, wispy, defeated idealism.

SECTION I (Lines 1-74)

Literally translated, the epigraph reads:

If I thought that my answer were to one who ever could return to the world; this flame should quake no more; but since none ever did return alive from this depth, if what I hear be true, without fear of infamy I answer thee.

The passage is from the *Inferno,* XXVII, lines 61-66, and, as noted, refers to the torture of Guido da Montefeltro in the eighth circle. In addition to the implications suggested, the use of this passage implies that the lovesong itself is not sung in the real world. The "lovesong" is actually the lament of a being divided between passion and timidity. The poem is an interior monologue; that is, Prufrock is speaking to himself in a kind of daydream. It opens with a command to the self (you) to accompany the physical him (I) to a distant "room." Apparently, the object of the journey is to declare his love to a lady. There are, however, "women" in the room, and it is never clear which one of this plurality is implied. It is possible that Prufrock characteristically has not made up his mind, or that it doesn't matter which one is involved. The opening image of the patient suggests Prufrock's view of himself as helpless—

etherized. The following images are sordid; they suggest the pointlessness of Prufrock's search. The time is evening – teatime. The "one-night cheap hotels" suggest fruitless unsatisfying sexual relations in the past. The "sawdust restaurants with oyster-shells" suggest cheap jerry-built (sawdust) places with shell ashtrays, and simultaneously begin the sea imagery which becomes significant later in the poem. The area to be traversed is a slum. The "tedious argument of insidious intent" recalls the epigraph and its victim condemned for perverting human reason by guile. The "you" is instructed not to ask "What is it?" but to "go and make our visit," The *visit* again suggests the decorous quality of Prufrock's personality. Arriving at the "room," he finds that the women are talking of Michelangelo – probably tediously. Michelangelo is a figure to whose strength and greatness Prufrock cannot aspire. From the dismal prospects of the "visit," Prufrock distracts himself by contemplating the yellow fog. This eight-line passage is dominated by sibilant sounds which re-enforce the tone and which contrast with the harsher sounds of the next twelve lines. Having distracted himself with the fog, he persuades himself that he has time "to prepare a face" for whatever he will be called upon to do; that is, either to make small talk over the tea table or to "murder and create." He takes great comfort in time, saying hypnotically, again and again, "there will be time..." He is putting off the "question" because he is timid and hesitant. But his mind is called back to the thought of the women, and the exact repetition of the previous wording re-enforces the idea of tediousness in their talk. This recurrent thought of the women leads him to speculate about their reaction to his physical self. He is aware of his baldness – aging, loss of sexual potency – and his thinness. There is an interesting contrast between self-images in this passage. On the one hand, he views himself as rather attractive – he describes his morning coat, his collar, his necktie "rich and modest," but simultaneously recognizes that the women may comment on the thinness of his arms and legs. And it is at this point that he allows himself the first sense of doubt – "do I dare disturb the universe?" His timidity and self-consciousness preclude his taking any action, regardless of desire. This realization in turn leads him to reveal his distaste for women as they are (in his objective reality). He has "measured out his life with coffee spoons." The tedium and monotony of all his previous experience begins to build in him the tension of action as opposed to inaction – the sense of frustration – and the next several lines indicate the increase of tension. He rejects the eyes and recoils from the horror of being "pinned" down and dissected like a grasshopper who "spits out" his life. He rejects the arms, but at the same time he parenthetically mentions them in an erotic context. He cannot think of any formula for his proposal, and he reveals his insecurity again and again in the repeated "how should I presume." Then, in the climactic passage, which serves also as a preamble to the remainder of the poem, he mentions the only possibility for him, a possibility which is humiliating in its presumptuous obsequiousness. It is important to note that the passage ends with a mark of elision, an indication that it is not completed, that it trails off into silence. The passage recalls the images in the first lines. The section ends with his wish that he had been "a pair of ragged claws," an idea which recalls the sea imagery of the first few lines. Prufrock sees that he lacks the mindless craving that could have placed him on terms with the reality of his situation and permitted him to survive in the depths where he exists unnaturally.

SECTION II (Lines 75-110)

Prufrock has already compared the fog to a cat. Now, in his reverie, he refers to the afternoon, quickly correcting himself to evening, as sleeping peacefully. Perhaps, he says, it malingers, as he does in his etherized state. Again, he confronts the difficulty of action. For him this difficulty is an outgrowth of a fear of personal inadequacy. His reverie reaches a climax as he compares himself to John the Baptist. For him, being beheaded may be a sign of being unmanned. Having made the comparison, he immediately denies the dignity of it. "I am no prophet," and furthermore he has seen the moment of his "greatness flicker." He considers himself the butt of a "footman," and this footman also represents death. Prufrock has confessed his cowardice to himself, and with the confession comes the awareness that it is too late for him to act—in fact it has always been too late for him. The tension of the last section of part one has been relaxed in this section, marked by a return to somnolent imagery.

From this point, the poem moves toward the closing image of drowning, which is the conclusion of the sea imagery begun with the oyster shells of the first lines, and the ragged claws of the end of the first section. From this point, Prufrock speaks constantly of what *would* have happened had it not been too late. His speculation leads him to the conclusion that the result would not have been in his favor anyway. The lines ending with "That is not what I meant at all" show his fear of being misunderstood, of having his proposal, his "overwhelming question" meet with casual rejection. The friction of these impossibilities against his decorousness, and the fear of being revealed, cause him to disclaim his pretensions and to rationalize his failure.

SECTION III (Lines 111-131)

In this final section the tone changes again. There is no more overwhelming question. The pace of the section is much more rapid, and the passage itself is much more lyric. He recognizes that he cannot even compare himself with Hamlet, but rather with Polonius, a sometime wise fool. He resolves to retreat to the beach, and like an ivy-league undergraduate, in white flannel trousers with the bottoms rolled, concern himself with questions no more momentous than "Shall I part my hair behind? Do I dare to eat a peach?" Parting his hair thus will perhaps hide the baldness—his age—and eating a peach is as near the forbidden fruit as he dares to approach.

The mermaids who tempted Ulysses will not sing to him. His conception of them has been a delusion. Delusions, however, are hard to dispel, and he invokes his in one final erotic, lyric cry. Then, like the sailors of myth seduced by the mermaids to their death, he is recalled to reality by the voices in the drawing room, and he awakens from his reverie too late. But there is no final struggle. All effort to action has disappeared, and his acceptance of the death of the inner life is completely passive.

"Prufrock" is a poem of dejection. The pose that Eliot adapts in this poem is interesting. The "voice" of the poem is the voice of an old man; yet, Eliot was less than thirty years old when he wrote it. The voice of age becomes a device typical of much of Eliot's verse. The basic concern with the destruction of the sensitive individual by the surrounding sordidness and by the perversion of ancient values is a theme that Eliot was to explore again and again. "Prufrock" was the best of Eliot's early poetry. He thought so himself, and said so in a letter to Harriet Monroe, editor of the journal *Poetry* in which "Prufrock" first appeared. In this poem, Eliot not only introduced some ideas with which he was to be concerned again and again, but he also introduced the device of the borrowed line in a new context. The following lines are either clear borrowings or are so close as obviously and intentionally to recall the original:

Line	Phrase	Source
29	"works and days of hands…"	Hesoid
52	"…voices dying with a dying fall…"	Shakespeare
81	"…I have wept and fasted, wept and prayed…"	Matthew
89	"…Among the porcelain…"	Emily Dickenson "I cannot live with you"

Line	Phrase	Source
124	"...I have heard the mermaids singing each to each..."	John Donne
82-83	The reference to John the Baptist as a whole, of course, recalls the Biblical story with all its implications.	
92	"...squeezed the universe into a ball..."	Marvel "To His Coy Mistress"
94-95	The whole reference recalls two Biblical stories— the story of Lazarus risen from the dead, and second story of Dives and Lazarus.	
111-119	The whole reference to Hamlet recalls the play, the character of Hamlet, the character of Polonius, and the interplay between the two.	

In short, then, this technique of Eliot's depends on evocation. He employs images which are expected to evoke in his readers echoes of other works and other ideas, and these echoes are supposed to enrich the context of both Eliot's poem and the original. At the same time, however, this technique presupposes an awareness of the sources to which Eliot refers on the part of the reader. Obviously, for readers unfamiliar with the scope of Eliot's reading and the scope of his learning, the poetry may constitute something of a puzzle. This technique, now frequently imitated by other modern poets, has led some students to regard the bulk of modern poetry as a kind of game of anagrams. This is an error. While an awareness of the hidden references does undoubtedly enrich the poetry, it is not essential to an awareness of the poetry.

The Lovesong of J. Alfred Prufrock, as has been stated, may serve as a general introduction to the body of Eliot's work. More particularly, it serves as a splendid orientation to Eliot's best known poem, *The Waste Land.*

THE WASTE LAND

The Waste Land is probably Eliot's best known poem. It was first published in 1922, and by the 1940's it had become a standard in most anthologies of modern poetry. It has been studied by generations of students; in fact, for many students it has formed the first introduction to contemporary poetry. The poem is so well-known that its name has become a tag for Eliot and the group of poets who have followed him. This group is commonly known as the "Waste Land group."

Reduced to its simplest terms, the poem is a statement of the experience that drives a character to a fortune teller, of the fortune that is told, and of the unfolding of that fortune. This simple outline, however, is complicated and universalized by being set within the framework of the Fisher King legend. Eliot has attached a series of notes to this poem. These notes are intended to supply contexts for some of the more obscure references and quotations within the poem. In the introduction to these notes, Eliot writes:

> Not only the title, but the plan and a good deal of the incidental symbolism of the poem were suggested by Miss Jessie L. Weston's book on the Grail legend: *From Ritual to Romance.* Indeed, so deeply am I indebted, Miss Weston's book will elucidate the difficulties of the poem much better than my notes can do; and I recommend it (apart from the great interest of the book itself) to any who think such elucidation of the poem worth the trouble. To another work of anthropology I am indebted in general, one which has influenced our generation profoundly; I mean *The Golden Bough;* I have used especially the two volumes *Adonis, Attis, Osiris.* Anyone who is acquainted with these works will immediately recognize in the poem certain references to vegetation ceremonies.

The Fisher King legend, carefully studied by Miss Weston in its relation to the stories connected with the Holy Grail, is an ancient legend originally connected with a vegetation cycle explaining the seasons. Sir James Fraser, in *The Golden Bough,* has traced the vegetation myths into antiquity. The ancient peoples of Egypt and Greece explained the cycle of the seasons in relation to the death and rebirth of a god. The god died in the winter with the death of the vegetation and was reborn in the spring with the rebirth of the vegetation. The spring, the planting season, was often accompanied by religious ceremonies symbolizing the "planting" of the dead god in the soil along with the seed for the new crops. Among more primitive peoples, these rituals often involved orgastic sexual rituals as well as human sacrifice. The winter too had its rituals. The death of the year was, as noted above, associated sometimes with the actual death of a god, sometimes with the sexual maiming of the god. Again these rituals were accompanied by symbolic representations of the imagined events, and involved either human sacrifice or ritual maiming of a person selected to represent the god. Sir James Fraser pointed out vestiges of these ancient rituals still existing within the Christian world, and also indicated that the death and rebirth of Christ falls within the pattern of this ancient ritual. Miss Weston has been able to trace vestiges of the ancient ritual transformed into Christian terms in the stories connected with the quest for the Holy Grail. In some of the ancient versions of these stories, for example, the questor arrived in a country which was barren or waste. He discovered that the barrenness of the land was magically associated with the wounding of the king. In some cases, there was even some indication that the wounding was sexual. The questor had to heal the wounded king, often by undergoing some sort of trial, and the healing of the king resulted in the reburgeoning of the land. As the Grail stories become more modern, the overlay of Christian ideas becomes heavier, and the ancient ritualistic concepts were more deeply buried, but they persist into quite modern times. These ideas concerning the development of certain Christian concepts and rituals out of pagan antiquity, and the ideas concerning the relation of the Christ story with much older pagan fertility rites, caused a tremendous impact on the intellectual conceptions of the generation which spanned the end of the Nineteenth and the beginning of the Twentieth centuries.

It is important to remember that the literal interpretation of Biblical evolution was held inviolable in the Anglo-European world for a thousand years. The end of the Nineteenth century saw a revolution in human thinking. Charles Darwin's *Origin of Species* appeared in 1859, offering a scientific theory of evolution. Anthropology began to demonstrate, late in the Nineteenth century, that many concepts held to be mystically Christian were in reality extremely ancient ideas whose origin was buried deep in pre-history. The Victorian concept that "God's in his heaven and all's right with the world," that the world was in a state of perfection, had been challenged, and by the latter half of the Nineteenth century the distrust of the old ideas had spread into literature. Matthew Arnold, in "Dover Beach," raised some of the questions that were plaguing the Victorian mind. Thomas Hardy in England, and Dostoyevsky in Russia, were introducing a new view of the human being operating in a universe which was essentially hostile to him, rather than in a universe dominated by an anthropomorphic God who was concerned even with the fall of a sparrow. The literary school called *Naturalism* developed in France and spread to America and elsewhere. This intellectual furor was culminated early in the Twentieth century by the First World War which provided positive proof of "Man's inhumanity to Man," and which indeed left many of those who survived it with a bitter feeling that they were quite alone in the universe—in a universe in which chaos was the natural order of things. Early in the Twentieth century, the philosophical groundwork for various philosophies of despair and dissolution had been laid, and by mid-century, after the added impetus of the second World War, such movements as the Beat and the Existentialist began to reach their full maturity.

Eliot's view of the world, his wasteland derogation of possibilities, was exactly right for the period after World War I. He became the spokesman in verse for that generation, as Ernest Hemingway became its spokesman in prose fiction. In *The Waste Land* Eliot overtly contrasts the glories of the past with the sordidness of the present. An interesting illustration of this occurs in section II (A Game of Chess) in which the first 33 lines (77-110) describe ancient grandeur while the following 61 lines (111-172) describe a modern situation. Many other illustrations of the contrast exist in the poem, sometimes within a single section and sometimes reaching from an idea developed in one section to a distantly removed image in another section. Since the poem depends for much of its effect on these contrasts, it is important to be aware of them and to be alert for them. Some will be illustrated in the detailed discussion which follows.

The poem is an extremely difficult one exactly because of the numerous interruptions in the narrative level and because of the piled up contrasts. In fact, the poem may be read on many levels. It has a narrative level, a story covering roughly a twelve hour period in a single day. Like "Prufrock" it is a kind of monologue containing within it snatches of dialogue remembered. It is also in the stream of consciousness; that is, like "Prufrock," its principal action occurs in the mind of the speaker rather than in the "real" world. The literature of the early Twentieth century is filled with experiments with what might be called the "internal monologue"; that is, with the free association of ideas in the mind of the narrator. James Joyce experimented with this concept in *Ulysses* and in *Finnegan's Wake;* Virginia Wolfe and William Faulkner are other well-known experimenters with this form. Since the association of ideas and the accompanying tangential flights of thought are instantaneous, these writers also had to experiment with the concepts of time. The philosophical experimentation of Henri Bergson, the French philosopher, had set the stage for much of this experimentation with time. In earlier fiction, for example, the time covered was commonly quite long. The novel *Tom Jones,* for example, covers some twenty years. Other novels cover the particular years of a series of events, or the cycle of a single life, or even the cycle of several generations. All these novels cover time lapses in the external world — that is, they are concerned with "clock time." But Einstein's theory of relativity suggests that there is no such thing as absolute time. Time is relative. Bergson further suggests that there are two kinds of time: relative time in the mathematical sense and relative time in the human sense. Every human being knows that a given period of clock time may appear longer or shorter depending upon the circumstances. A period spent pleasurably is likely to seem to fly, while a period spent painfully is likely to seem endless. That these circumstances are real enough is illustrated by idioms in the language; idioms like "time flies," and "time stands still."

In the physical world, any given event occupies a measurable quantity of clock time, but in the world of the mind, time is not measurable; rather, it is relative to events. Some events "endure" for a considerable time, while other events have a very brief duration. Experiments with the reproduction of thought patterns necessitated experiments with duration in the human rather than in the clock sense. Quite a number of contemporary works cover extremely brief periods of time—in some cases, matters of minutes—instead of the years or decades commonly employed in nineteenth century and earlier fiction. (It is not to be assumed that *all* contemporary literature is removed from events in terms of clock time; in fact, most detective stories are based upon a rather close attention to chronological time. Many other works, even many of quite respectable literary reputation, are concerned with chronological time.) For example, *The Catcher in the Rye* is a novel that may serve to illustrate an interesting use of time. That novel is framed between two scenes in which the narrator is telling a story to a psychiatrist in a mental hospital in California. The telling time is roughly equivalent to the time it takes the reader to read the book. But within the narration, the narrator is speaking about a period covering four days of chronological time. And within that literal level, the narrator's reaction of certain events makes them appear longer in terms of human time than they actually were in terms of clock time by the simple expedient of remembering more details about these particular events and skimming over other events.

In *The Waste Land,* then, Eliot experiments with both the idea of human time and with the stream of consciousness. To complicate the matter, he employs a number of quotations which are not in English. The first of these, the epigraph, is taken from the *Satiricon* of Petronius (Chapter 48). Then, in the first section, there is some German, and later in the poem some French, and even some Sanscrit. Beyond that, a number of lines are quoted from literary works in English. All of this tends to confuse the reader if he fails to remember the importance of the juxtaposition of the present and the past in the poem. But beyond this, the quotations are intended to bring into a new context, ideas which have appeared elsewhere. These are lines recollected by the speaker, and they serve to establish a suggested context into which, or perhaps through which, his immediate thinking may operate. Further, it serves to universalize, or internationalize, the context; that is, the "truth" of the poem transcends time and place. It has existence in all times and in all places, or in no time and in no place. Many of the quotations employed are identified in the notes provided at the end of the poem. It is wise for the reader to take the trouble to look up the original sources, because in many instances the context of the lines in this poem are influenced or clarified by the original context.

Eliot's technique in *The Waste Land* consists of the juxtaposition of extreme contemporaneousness with mysticism and religious symbolism derived from the past. The poem abounds with illustrations of the juxtaposing of past and present on many levels. The structure of the poem is built out of the contrasts in time, of which the most obvious and ironically dramatic are the series of "scenes" from modern life set against the memories of myths related in *The Golden Bough* and *From Ritual to Romance*. These contrasts are supported and universalized by Eliot's use of literary reminiscence and reference. The poem illustrates Eliot's conception of the past as an active part of the present and his belief that disparate materials drawn from the past may be fused into a new creation which in turn has a validity of its own.

Since this is the stated aim of the poem, the use of time may provide part of the key to the understanding of the poem. On the superficial level, the poem gives the feeling that time stands still, that there is a duration. But the essence of the poem achieves a sense of timelessness. The chanting of "Shantih" [the peace that passeth understanding] at the close of the poem indicates that for Eliot "peace" can come only as a dimension of duration. On the literal level, the poem covers a twelve-hour period in a single day. In this sense, its relation with the *Ulysses* of James Joyce is apparent. The literal time changes are indicated in the following lines:

61	"Under the brown fog of a winter dawn..."
208	"Under the brown fog of a winter noon..."
220	"At the violet hour, the evening hour..."

But at the same time, this day has a cosmic dimension; it is a millenium. The poem illustrates the concept of the eternal return of the same. Consecutively, the poem has imposed upon it, on still another level of comprehension, a cycle of birth, growth, maturity, decay, death, rebirth— reiterating the theme of eternal return.

According to Eliot's own analysis of the poem, Tiresias is the central character, and what Tiresias sees is the substance of the poem. Now

Tiresias has not only seen and experienced these events in the past, but he has also foretold them in the future and already foresuffered them. If this is the case, then the future coexists with the present and the past. Furthermore, Eliot says that all the other characters in the poem merge into Tiresias. Tiresias is a hermaphrodidic blind seer: "I Tiresias, though blind, throbbing between two lives,/ Old man with wrinkled female breasts..." In his notes, Eliot writes:

> Just as the one-eyed merchant, seller of currants, melts into
> The Phoenician Sailor, and the latter is not wholly distinct from
> Ferdinand Prince of Naples, so all the women are one woman, and
> the two sexes meet in Tiresias.

If all the men blend into one man, and all the women into one woman, and the sexes meet in Tiresias, then Tiresias is himself a condensed history of man; or, in other words, a brief history contained within a single individual of the fall of man. Tiresias provides an aesthetic unity and continuity for the poem in addition to functioning to unify past, present, and future.

But Tiresias is also blind. Therefore, he appears to represent the eye of the mind, or a kind of universal contemplative consciousness. This inner reality subsists through all the experiences that he "sees," and serves to unite past and present, men and women, the characters in the poem and the "I" who is the speaker.

As noted above, Eliot states that what Tiresias "sees" is the substance of the poem. Tiresias comprehends that the only salvation is death, because out of death comes rebirth. Death and rebirth constitute a cycle of eternal return, and a cycle of eternal return is a manifestation of the duration of time. Time, then, appears to be at the center of Tiresias' vision, but the time that he sees is not a chronological time. It is a timeless time, a time of indefinite duration.

The poem is filled with a multitude of symbols, each of which exist on a variety of experiential levels. The number of levels that a given reader can perceive depends upon the readers' knowledge and background. Eliot intends the reader, within the limitations of his experience, to associate the multiplicity of images freely. The richness of this texture permits Eliot to intermingle literary levels and temporal levels; to mingle past, present, and future in a continuum of NOW. In *The Function of Criticism*, Eliot wrote:

The existing [literary] monuments form an ideal order among themselves, which is modified by the introduction of the new (the really new) work of art among them. The existing order is complete before the new work arrives; for the order to persist after the supervention of the novelty, the *whole* existing order must be, if ever so slightly, altered; and so the relations, proportions, values of each work of art toward the whole are readjusted; and this is the conformity between the old and the new.

The Waste Land illustrates the conformity between the old and the new in a single literary creation. Obviously, it is an extremely difficult piece of work. These many threads are difficult to trace through the whole tapestry.

The following sections will attempt to show some of the relations within the poem, but it must be understood that no brief analysis like the following can possibly hope to illustrate or illuminate all of the possible interrelations within this extremely complex structure. The student will need to bring to the reading all of his own experience and intuition as well as whatever help he can get.

SECTION I – THE BURIAL OF THE DEAD

The epigraph is, as noted above, from the *Satiricon* of Petronius. "With my own eyes I saw the Sibyl suspended in a glass bottle at Cumae, and when the boys said to her 'Sibyl, what is the matter?' she would always respond: 'I yearn to die.'" Petronius' work belongs to the first century A. D. Petronius is talking within his work of a period much anterior to his own. The speaker says "With my own eyes," indicating that he was physically present at the event. But he says that he "saw" the Sibyl; in other words, he is describing an event that for him took place in his past. In this quotation, the time shifts in a number of directions:

FROM		*TO*	
	The reader's present		Eliot's present (reader's past)
	Eliot's present		Petronius's present (Eliot's past)
	Petronius' present		the Sibyl's present (Petronius's past)

The reader is free to move through these past-present interrelationships as he chooses. But the situation is further complicated by the facts of the story of the Sibyl. The Sibyl was an oracle granted perpetual life but not perpetual youth, so that while she lived centuries, as she grew older she shrank, finally to the size of a grasshopper. Thus, the Sibyl is timeless, but simultaneously caught in the "human time trap" because she ages but she cannot die. Because she cannot die, it is quite impossible for her to be reborn. She is removed from both the cycle of time and the cycle of birth-death-rebirth. Since the epigraph contains all these suggestions of time level as well as the substance of the poem, it is well chosen to introduce the poem.

The second quotation, addressed to Ezra Pound, simply calls him the "better craftsman." Eliot and Pound were close friends. After Eliot had finished the manuscript of *The Waste Land,* he gave it to Pound to read. Pound edited the poem, reducing it to about half of its original length and apparently tightening and strengthening it in the process. Eliot dedicates the poem to Pound as an expression of his gratitude for Pound's efforts.

The opening line of the poem places the poem in time. April is the *now* of the poem. The literal plot line of the poem occurs in April. This time level exists within the time level of the section. The section title, "The Burial of the Dead," recalls the Egyptian ritual of Osiris, a fertility ritual normally taking place in the Spring. April, the time of the poem, is the Easter month, evoking the concepts associated with the death and resurrection of the Christ. Thus the fertility rites are immediately introduced into the poem, and the major thematic strain is initiated in the title of the first section and its juxtaposition with the first line.

In the eighth line, with the mention of the Starnbergersee, Eliot introduces a locale. This·lake, and the Hofgarten two lines later, are located in Munich. The recalled snatches of conversation of this passage move the reader into a past-present no-time. The line, "when we were children," suggests a past for the speaker. The whole setting, and especially the line in German ["I am not Russian, I come from Lithuania, pure German."] suggest the rootlessness of the persons concerned. They are from nowhere; they live everywhere. The passage evokes the idea of the generation after World War I; a rootless generation drifting around Europe with no particular direction and no particular ambition. Characters like these abound in the fiction of Hemingway, F. Scott Fitzgerald, and other chroniclers of the time.

At line 19, the waste land imagery is resumed from the first line of the poem. There is "stony rubbish," "dead trees," "dry stone," and "no sound of water," The Son of man reference suggests a Biblical context. This is reinforced by the echo of Ecclesiastes in line 23. The red rock is something of a mystery, but one critic sees it as a reference to the Mount of Purgatory from the third canto of Dante's *Purgatorio*. The "handful of dust" in line 30 is both a death image [Dust thou art and to dust thou shalt return.] and a suggestion that the dust may become fruitful soil with the help of spring rain which comes in April. The following lines in German are from the Sailor's Song in *Tristan und Isolde:* "Fresh blow the wind/ From off the bow,/ My Irish maid,/ Where lingerest thou?" Fresh wind and the sea are both in contrast with heat and dryness in the preceding lines.

The next seven lines, in English, revert to the past tense introduced in lines eight through sixteen and culminate the recalled conversation of those lines. The last two lines of the English passage introduce for the first time into the poem the second thematic strain, the concept of time suspended in infinity. The speaker is "neither living nor dead," but suspended between the two. He is "looking into the heart of light"; that is, he is at the still point of the universe where everything becomes one with The One. The final line of this passage reverts to German. It is another line from *Tristan und Isolde:* "Desolate and empty the sea." It is intended as a conclusion to the earlier song, but it is also antiphonal to the song since it has both a different rhythm (no longer lyrical) and a different implication. Desolation is a characteristic of the waste land.

The next passage changes time once more into the immediate past-present. Madam Sosostris is a clairvoyant, an oracle, and suggests an identity with the Sibyl of the epigraph. She tells a fortune, (lines 46-56) and the working out of this fortune constitutes the plot structure of the poem. Multiple time shifts are implied in the section, since the clairvoyant may be identified with the Sibyl, since line 48 is from Shakespeare's *The Tempest,* and since the Tarot cards are believed to be of ancient Egyptian origin and are attributed to Thoth, counselor of Osiris who was King of Egypt. Furthermore, the names of the cards (Phoenician Sailor, Belladonna, the man with three staves, the Wheel, the one-eyed merchant, The Hanged Man) suggest the characters of the poem. The "Lady of the Rocks" recalls the red rock of line 25, and the "something...which I am forbidden to see" is perhaps the "something different" of line 27. Madam Sosostris, who has a name suggesting a Greco-Egyptian origin, is a modern vulgarized version of the Egyptian magicians who professed to control fertility and to forecast the rise and fall of the waters of the Nile through the symbols of the Tarot cards. But Madam Sosostris in the poem is an astrologer, the kind of person we are likely to regard as a fraud in the twentieth century. The shifts in time here are important. A fortune, a prediction of the *future,* is told in the poem's present by a woman who suggests both the Greek *past* (Petronius) and the Egyptian *past* (Tarot cards) and who uses an Elizabethan reference *(The Tempest).* The *future* is foretold in the *present* tense employing a vehicle, the cards, which belongs to the *past.* Within the fortune, the key line is "Fear death by water." Such a death may result either from too much water (drowning) or not enough water, as the land dies and becomes waste when there is no water.

The last passage of the first section occurs in the present of the poem: "Under the brown fog of a winter *dawn."* Eliot states in his notes that the opening line of this section is derived from Baudelaire's verse ["Swarming city, city full of dreams,/ where specters in full day grasp passersby."] while line 63 owes its meaning to Dante ["...an endless train/ Of shades so numerous I scarce believe/ That death had claimed so many for his own."] as does line 64 ["Herein so far as I could judge by ear/ No lamentations were there—any sighs/ Which moved to trembling the timeless air."] thus, the "unreal city" is in one sense at least a city of the dead. The city is real enough, clearly identified as London. The reference to the flat note on the ninth stroke of the clock in the tower of the church of Saint Mary Woolnoth, while Eliot explains it as something he has experienced many times and associates with London, also suggests the line "and there was a darkness over all the earth until the ninth hour" [Luke, 23:44]. The paradoxical reference to "Stetson...in the ships/ at Mylae" implies a multilevel shift in time reference. *Stetson* appears to be a name associated with the Twentieth century. It frankly recalls the trade name of a hat. The second part of the reference involves a battle of the Punic Wars (260 B.C.). The war was fought between the Romans and the Cartheginians, but the word *Punic,* from the Latin *Poeni,* means *Phoenician,* and the reference evokes the drowned Phoenician sailor of the fortune. The conversation in lines 71-75 envokes memories of the Egyptian fertility rites as discussed in *The Golden Bough* while the last two lines of this passage are a parody of a dirge sung by Cornelia, the mother of Marcello, over her dead son in Act V scene iv of John Webster's *The White Devil,* a play printed in 1612.

> Call for the robin redbreast and the wren,
> Since o'er shady groves they hover,
> And with leaves and flowers do cover
> The friendless bodies of unburied men.
> Call unto his funeral dole
> The ant, the field mouse, and the mole,
> To rear him hillocks that shall keep him warm,
> And, when gay tombs are robbed, sustain no harm;
> But keep the wolf far thence, that's foe to men,
> For with his nails he'll dig them up again.

Eliot substitues "Dog" for "wolf," perhaps intending to refer to Sirius, the dog star as well as to parody Webster. Sirius appears at dawn in the east just about the time of the Summer Solstice when the Nile begins to rise. The Egyptians called it *Sothis,* the Star of Isis. The star was considered to be the goddess of life come to mourn her lover and to wake him from the dead. Literally, the conversation with Stetson is an enactment of the lines from Baudelaire which open the passage — ghosts converse with passers-by in broad daylight. The passage closes with another line from Baudelaire: "hypocrite reader — my similacrum — my brother." The reader is identified into the poem and with the other personages.

The movement of the whole of the first section, like that of the poem itself, is psychological rather than chronological. The tortured questioning of the protagonist, the fleeting associations, and the semi-hysterical horror and confusion of response, as the protagonist faces the "cruellest month" and its implications give the section a movement closely resembling stream of consciousness. Time, as experience, has the quality of flowing, and this quality is an enduring base within the constant flux and movement of time as chronology. The quality of duration is superimposed on incessant change. Water, particularly flowing water, as in a river, is the perfect and conventional symbol for the flow of time. The waste land is similarly a perfect symbol for the cessation of time — for timelessness. Stream of consciousness is the literary technique which makes possible the dissolution of chronological time and the introduction of time flux.

SECTION II — A GAME OF CHESS

The second section of the poem is called "A Game of Chess." The title is borrowed from a play, by Thomas Middleton (1624), in which the action is symbolically played out as moves in a game of chess. The game is very ancient, having originated in India, perhaps as long as 4000 years ago. It came to Europe via Persia probably in the eleventh century, and during the middle ages acquired some of the symbolism also associated with the Quest for the Holy Grail.

The opening lines of the section are from Shakespeare's *Antony and Cleopatra:*

The barge she sat in, like a burnish'd throne
burnt on the water. ...(Act II, scene ii, line 196)

But Eliot makes a significant change by substituting *Chair* for *barge,* and thereby evoking the story of Cassiopeia and the whole Andromeda legend which is a "waste land" legend. Line 82 introduces the "seven branched candelabra" which may be a reference to the constellation of the Pleiades (or seven sisters) which is located next to the constellation of Cassiopeia. The seven branched candelabra is also associated with the Menorah of Judaic tradition [see Zechariah IV:2, I Kings VII:49, Exodus XXV:37, Revelations IV:5] which in turn is associated with a winter solstice festival and with a victory over the Maccabees. If Eliot intended a reference to the Menorah, then a reference to the apocryphal *First Book of the Maccabees* may be suggested:

And behold, our sanctuary, even our beauty and our glory, is laid waste, and the Gentiles have profaned it.

The "laquearia" of line 92 is derived from the *Aeneid,* Book I, line 726: *"Dependent lychni laquearibus aureis/ Incensi..."* ["Lamps hang from fretted roofs of gold/ burning..."] Line 98 is derived from Milton's Paradise Lost, IV, 140: "...and overhead up-grew/ Insuperable highth of loftiest shade,/ Cedar, and pine, and fir, and branching palm,/ A sylvan scene..." The Philomela story cited in lines 99-101 Eliot derives from Ovid's version, told in the *Metamorphosis.* The carved dolphin in line 96 may be a reference to early Christian art in which the dolphin symbolized diligence or love.

The point, however, lies in the richness of the whole passage. The lavish opulence of legendary queens like Dido, Cassiopeia, Cleopatra, and Philomela is evoked throughout the passage. The remainder of the section reproduces a contemporary pub conversation involving several women and a discussion of false teeth, pregnancy, and possibly an abortion. The tone of this latter half of the section is nervous, jazzy, slangy, and routine. The passage contains relatively few allusions. Line 118 refers again to Webster's play, and line 138 to the chess game in Thomas Middleton's play, *Women Beware Women* (1657). Line 115 anticipates a reference in section III of *The Waste Land,* and line 126 recalls line 48 of Part I, the line from the *Tempest* which occurs in the fortune referring to the drowned Phoenician sailor. The last line of the section is from Ophelia's mad song in Shakespeare's *Hamlet,* Act IV, scene i. The section divides into two parts at line 110. The contrast between the two parts is striking. The vitality of the contemporary women in part two is like that of the queens on a chess board as contrasted to that of those women who sat on "burnished thrones." The games of contemporary women are as chess games, an empty pastime or at best an open hostility ending in stalemate, compared with the depth of feeling and suffering of the Philomelas of antiquity. In the second part of the section, the nightingale sings in a "desert," and the "sylvan scene" has become "withered stumps of time."

The "'Jug Jug' to dirty ears" anticipates the next section. The contrasting passage is modern in its idiom. No longer does the nightingale sing. Now it is "O O O O that Shakespeherian Rag" that fills "all the desert with inviolable voice." The water imagery is reiterated, but without potency, in "hot water at ten./ And if it rains, a closed car at four." The life-giving rain must now be escaped in a closed car. The conversation is constantly interrupted by the pub keepers "Hurry up please its time" — time to go home. There is a sense of urgency in the words. The conversation is not concluded. It is simply disrupted by closing time. A choice is implied but never made because there isn't time. Time runs out on these people. The ancient fertility symbols occur in the passage, but in an emasculated form, negated by the vulgar insensitivity of the modern world. The parting goodnights of these ladies melt into Ophelia's mad parting. Ophelia's is another death by water, but it is self-destructive. It is not a baptism or the preparation for a rebirth.

SECTION III — THE FIRE SERMON

The Fire Sermon belongs to an oriental tradition. In the Fire Sermon, the Buddha explains to the priests that all things which are received as impressions through the physical senses or through the mind are actually on fire. The ritual requires that the priests ask about the nature of the fire and that the explanation is that things burn with the fires of passion, hatred, infatuation, birth, death, sorrow, lamentation, misery, grief, and despair. Fire is also a traditional part of the midsummer festivals of earlier western civilizations.

The section opens with a reference to Edmund Spenser's *Prothalamion* (1596):

> There, in a Meadow, by the Riuers side,
> A flocke of *Nymphes* I chaunced to espy,
> All louely Daughters of the Flood thereby,
> With goodly greenish locks all loose vyntyde,
> As each had bene a Bryde,
> And each one had a little wicker basket,
> Made of fine twigs entrayled curiously,
> In which they gathered flowers to fill their flasket:
> And with fine Fingers, cropt full feateously
> The tender stalkes on hye.
> Of euery sort, which in that Meadow grew,
> They gathered some; the Violet pallid blew,

> The little dazie, that at euening closes,
> The virgin Lillie, and the Primrose trew,
> With store of vermeil Roses,
> To decke their Bridegromes posies,
> Against the Brydale day, which was not long:
>> Sweete Themmes runne softly, till I end my Song.

The last line forms the refrain for each of the stanzas of this long "marriage poem." But the reference is used here for contrast; the nymphs are departed, and "sweet Thames" is full of the leavings of promiscuity and modern life. Line 182 evokes Psalm 137: "By the rivers of Babylon, there we sat down, yea, we wept..." *Leman* is a lake near Geneva in Switzerland, but the word also means an illicit lover. The next two lines recall Spenser's poem again, and the following two are echoes of Andrew Marvell's poem "To His Coy Mistress" (1621-1678):

> But at my back I always hear
> Time's winged chariot hurrying near,
> And yonder all before us lie
> Deserts of vast eternity.

Here it is not "Time's winged chariot," but "The rattle of bones"; it is death none the less.

Lines 187 to 195 are a statement of the Fisher King myth, derived directly from Jessie Weston's *From Ritual to Romance,* but modernized by placing the fishing king beside a "dull canal...behind the gashouse." Line 192 again evokes Shakespeare's *Tempest* (Act I, scene ii). Ferdinand, just escaped from the sea, finds himself on a desert island. He thinks he hears music:

> Where should this music be? i' th' air or th' earth?
> It sounds no more! And sure it waits upon
> Some god o' th' island; sitting on a bank,
> Weeping again the king my father's wrack,
> This music crept by me upon the waters,
> Allaying both their fury and my passion
> With its sweet air; Thence I have followed it —
> Or it hath drawn me rather — but 'tis gone.
> No, it begins again.

Then Ferdinand hears Ariel, a spirit, singing this song:

> Full fathoms five thy father lies;
> Of his bones are coral made;
> Those are pearls that were his eyes:
> Nothing of him that doth fade,
> But doth suffer a sea change
> Into something rich and strange
> Sea nymphs hourly ring his knell.

In short, Shakespeare's play is concerned with still another "death by water."

Lines 196-97 recall both Marvell's passage, already quoted above, and Day's *Parliament of Bees.* Eliot provides these lines in his own notes. Lines 198 to 201 bring into the poem a character named Sweeney whom Eliot has used in other poems before *The Waste Land;* "Sweeney Among the Nightingales" and "Sweeney Agonistes." He is a hairy ape; the epitome of vulgarity in modern man. Mrs. Porter and her daughter are heroines of a pornographic Anzac marching song probably sung to the tune of "Pretty Red Wing." The passage ends with a French line: "And O the voices of children singing in the cupola." This line, from Verlaine's *Parsifal,* suggests the Grail legends directly. The contrasts in this passage are more immediate than in section II, but their tone is similar. The vulgarity and shallowness of the modern is contrasted with the beauty, simplicity, and depth of the past. What was once ritualistic and meaningful is now empty and only dirty. But it is impossible to assume that Eliot is merely invoking the "good old days" in preference to modernity.

The brief four-line passage which follows is rich in connotation. Obviously, it is intended to recall the earlier passage, in section II which deals with Philomela (lines 99-103). The connection is established through the repetition of "Jug jug..." But this brief passage also owes a debt to Trico's song from John Lyly's *Alexander and Campaspe* (1584). The text of the play appears to be irrelevant to the point here, but the words of Trico's song recall the Philomela lengend:

> What bird so sings, yet does so wail?
> O! 'tis the ravished nightengale.
> Jug, Jug, Jug, Jug, Tereu, she cries,
> And still her woes at midnight rise.

The passage serves as a striking contrast to Mrs. Porter and her daughter. It is immediately followed by a return to the immediate now of the poem. Something like five or six hours of chronological time are represented by the preceding 200 lines.

Mr. Eugenides, the one-eyed Smyrna merchant, chanting the ritual of commercial translation, is closely related to the one-eyed merchant of the fortune told in section I (lines 46-56). He issues an invitation to indulge in promiscuous pleasures. It is possible that he may be an exponent of a "cult" of sexual perversion. Apparently in his implied bisexuality, he also serves as a lesser anticipation of Tiresias who appears on the scene just a few lines later. His name itself is suggestive of *eugenics,* the science of improving the qualities of the race by the careful selection of parents. The presence of such a suggestion in his name is obviously intended to be ironic. He may also be intended as a contrast to Tereus, the villain of the Philomela legend. Jessie Weston has a brief note in her book about Syrians in the ancient world. She says:

> As ardently religious as practically business-like, the Syrians introduced their native deities wherever they penetrated, "founding their chapels at the same time as their countinghouses." (p. 160)

Tiresias is the most important personage in the poem. As has been noted, he unites within himself all the personages of the poem. It is significant that he is introduced at the exact center of the poem: this passage runs from line 215 to line 248; the exact middle of the poem (433 lines) falls at line 217; the exact middle of section III (148 lines) falls at line 247, and section III is the middle section of the five sections of the poem. Thematically, the climax of the poem falls within this passage.

On the superficial level, the scene between the typist and the "young man carbuncular" is one more example of the debased attitude toward sexual relations between men and women in the contemporary society. It is the central irony of the section that it is not the *fire* of lust at all which is illustrated here; rather, what seems to be illustrated is an attitude of complete indifference toward chastity. Furthermore, Eliot seems to be evoking the ancient practice of "sanctified harlotry," as Fraser calls it. According to the old practice, a girl, in order to promote her own fertility, consorted with a stranger before her marriage. The ritual coupling was accompanied by a ritual feast and music.

Tiresias is a witness to the act, but he has foresuffered all and fore-seen all. He is a fortune teller too, like Madam Sosostris and the Cumaen Sibyl. As a mere spectator, Tiresias transcends the action of the poem and the time of the poem, for he brings together within his heterosexual self all the personages of the poem as he unites within the timelessness of his experience all the time levels of the poem. Eliot's own note on the signifi-cance of Tiresias has already been noted above. In that note, Eliot calls attention to a passage from Ovid's *Metamorphosis:*

> ...The woman's pleasure—Jove would have it so—
> Is greater than the man's. His wife said no.
> Tiresias (they concurred), who knew by test
> Both sides of love, would judge the issue best.
>   Once in the woods at mating-time he [Tiresias] broke
> On two huge serpents with his stick's rude stroke;
> And changed from man to woman at the blow,
> (A thing most strange) he passed seven seasons so.
> The eighth, he saw the selfsame pair, and cried:
> "If in your contact such strong spells reside,
> That whoso strikes, from sex to sex must go,
> I'll try the charm again," and, striking so,
> He felt the power, was changed again, and wore
> This time for good, the shape his mother bore.
>   So, called to judge the playful suit that day,
> He found for Jove, and Juno, so they say,
> Was vexed so deeply that, forgetting all
> Justice and reason in a thing so small,
> She made her chosen umpire feel her spite,
> Dooming his eyes to everlasting night.
> Almighty Jove (since no god can undo
> Another's work) gave him a vision new,
> The power to see events before they came,
> And soothed his sufferings with a prophet's fame.

Tiresias, then, qualified to judge the sexual act because he "knew by test both sides of love," points to two levels of meaning, and the flavor of the debased ritual is caught and emphasized by the formality of the rhyme used to describe its tawdriness. What Tiresias sees, the center of the poem, is the timeless quality of an action affected by time-wrought changes. But beyond that, what Tiresias sees, with the eye of the mind, is that the only salvation is death, because only out of that death can come a rebirth.

As usual, this passage contains a number of references and allusions. The first of these occurs at line 221. Eliot's notes identify his reference from a poem by Sappho, but the more obvious reference for most American readers would be Robert Louis Stevenson's *Requiem:* "Home is the sailor, home from the sea..." It is possible that the line "Out of the window perilously spread/ Her drying combinations touched by the sun's last rays..." may be an intentional mockery of Keats' line from the "Ode to a Nightingale" "Magic casements, opening on the foam/ Of perilous seas..." The next reference occurs in line 253, and it recalls Oliver Goldsmith's song, from the *Vicar of Wakefield* (Chapter 29):

> When lovely woman stoops to folly
>   And finds too late that men betray,
> What charm can soothe her melancholy,
>   What art can wash her guilt away?
> The only art her guilt to cover,
>   To hide her shame from every eye,
> To give repentance to her lover,
>   And wring his bosom — is to die.

This reference helps to point up the tawdriness and meaninglessness of chastity in the scene described. Line 257 recalls again the scene from Shakespeare's *The Tempest,* cited above. The "Magnus Martyr" of line 264 is a reference to a church interior designed by Christopher Wren, the eighteenth century architect.

At line 266, the song of the three Thames-daughters begins. They are a distortion both of the nymphs of Spenser's *Prothalamion* introduced in the first lines of section III and of the Rhine maidens of Wagner's *Gotterdammerung.* Once again a contrasting situation is created by the introduction of Elizabeth and Leicester in line 279 and the stated contrast between their barge and present day barges. Eliot quotes a source in his own notes for this passage. The song of the Thames-Daughters is both the music of the gramophone mentioned in line 256 and the "music [which] crept by me upon the waters" in line 257. At line 292, the three "daughters" sing separately, each telling her pitiful story. The whole scene is an echo of Dante's "La Pia." The song establishes the scene in *The Waste Land* as purgatorial, as it has earlier been suggested that the scene was in the *Inferno.* The purgatory, however, is worthless, since the suffering described is neither voluntary nor purposive. Each of the singers treats her loss of chastity as inevitable and as bound up with the very soil of the waste land. The river or the sea at the scene of violation has no cleansing power. Everything is meaningless, purposeless, unrelated, a part of the negation of life itself. The gramophone record stops with reiterated "la la" at the end of the song. All this, the pointless seduction, has already been foretold and foresuffered by Tiresias, by the typist and her young man, and in the fortune.

The mood of the Thames-daughters' song is shattered by the introduction of the words of St. Augustine. Eliot provides the passage in his own notes. In Carthage, Augustine heard "a cauldron of unholy loves" singing in his ears. But Carthage is the home of Dido, evoked in the first part of Section II. The unholy loves that Augustine heard were burning.

The section ends with works from the Fire Sermon immediately followed by another quotation from Augustine. The juxtaposition of what Eliot calls "these two representatives of eastern and western asceticism" at the close of the "Fire Sermon" serves to heighten the disparity between the "burning" of all things and the coldness and emptiness of the modern. The stories of the Thames-daughters contain no burning, no passion. Neither does the story of the secretary and her young man. The fire is put out by the complete indifference to the body and the spirit. Both Buddha and Christ taught that moral virtue was the means of achieving the supreme object of life, the eternal and timeless salvation of the individual soul. Eliot says in his notes that the Fire Sermon corresponds in importance to the Sermon on the Mount. Christ sought salvation in a blissful eternity while Buddha sought it in a final release from suffering through annihilation, but both conceived fire as a symbol for the destructive elements in life. The closing lines of the section echo Augustine's prayer that he may be a brand plucked from the burning, but the prayer is interrupted as the unfinished lines suggest. The broken prayer leads logically into the next section of the poem which suggests the possibility of purification, and purification with water, the antithesis of fire and the symbol of baptism which in turn prepares the road to rebirth.

SECTION IV – DEATH BY WATER

The title of the section indicates the fulfillment of the fortune told in section I. Phlebas the Phoenician is the equivalent of the drowned Phoenician sailor of the fortune and unites in himself the one-eyed merchant, Mr. Eugenides, Ferdinand, and all the others. The ancient fertility cults, according to Sir James Fraser, frequently consigned the effigy of the dead god to the sea and then welcomed it as reborn at the end of its journey when it was carried back by a predictable current. Thus, "As he rose and fell He passed the stages of his age and youth." On this level, the lines symbolize the relinquishing of "the natural man" to the "current under sea"; to the metamorphosis suggested by the line "picked his bones by whispers," which seems to suggest both the disintegration of the flesh, the old life, and the mystery, told in whispers, half-heard, of the new life. "Entering the whirlpool," in a moment of terrifying surrender, results, in the words of the Fire Sermon, in the peace of becoming "free of attachment." The protagonist is free of "the cry of gulls, and the deep sea swell." It is no longer necessary for him to measure life in terms of age and youth because he is free of chronological time and exists at the still point in a state of timelessness. The "Gentile or Jew" directly addressed in line 319 is derived from the Pauline Epistle to the Romans in which it is stated that the new life in Christ belongs equally to both:

> How shall we, that are dead to sin, live any longer therein? Know ye not, that so many of us as were baptized into Jesus Christ were baptized into his death? Therefore we are buried with him by baptism into death: that like as Christ was raised up from the dead by the glory of the Father, even so we also should walk in newness of life. (VI:2-4)

The "wheel" in line 320 is a multiple reference. On the one hand, it is the wheel of a ship, indicating a steersman steering. On another level, it is a reference to the wheel mentioned in the fortune in section I. Still further, it is the wheel of fortune, or the wheel of Buddhist doctrine, the wheel of resurrection. Section IV marks the end of the journey on the waters of Leman. The death by water foretold in the fortune in section I and foresuffered by various personages in sections II and III has now been realized in section IV, and the fortune has been fulfilled. Death and baptism have been linked in the words of St. Paul. The road to resurrection and rebirth has been prepared.

SECTION V – WHAT THE THUNDER SAID

The title of this section appears to be derived from the parable of the Thunder, an Indian myth from the Upanishads. In it, the supreme Lord of the Creation speaks through the thunder, answering the request of his offspring. In his notes Eliot states that the first passage of this section contains three themes: "The journey to Emmaus, the approach to the Chapel Perilous and the present decay of eastern Europe." The first is derived from Luke, XXIV:13-31, the section which recounts the resurrection. The second theme is taken from Jessie Weston's book. Miss Weston maintains that the Grail legends are, in part at least, accounts of initiations into cults employing a mystery ritual and claiming an actual knowledge of the future life. She suggests that the initiations existed on two levels: "the Lower, into the mysteries of generation, *i.e.,* of physical Life; the Higher, into the Spiritual Divine Life, where man is made one with God." (p. 182) Further, she believes that "the tradition of the Perilous Chapel, which survives in the Grail romances in confused and contaminated form, was a reminiscence of the test for this lower initiation." The third theme Eliot substantiates in his own note to lines 366-76 of the poem. The citation is from Hermann Hesse, and it states that at least half of Eastern Europe is already on its way to chaos. It goes along singing drunkenly in spiritual madness. The bourgeoise laugh at these songs; the saint and seer hear them with tears.

The opening lines of the section are an echo of lines 19-24 in section I. Obviously, too, this passage serves as an account of the crucifixion. St. Paul's linking of death and baptism at the close of section IV forms the starting point for section V. The Christian mystery of life through death is now linked with the vegetation myths. "He who was loving is now dead." The "He" is a combination of Christ, Attis, Adonis, Fisher King, Phlebas the Phoenician, etc. "We who were living are now dying" in the sense of the words of St. Paul cited above. Man, whose life was once enriched by the figures of faith, no longer responds to them. The speaker approaches the Chapel Perilous through a waste land more parched than any previously cited in the poem. "Here is no water." The rock imagery of the poem, introduced in the "red rock" of line 25, section I, reiterated in the fortune through "Belladonna, the Lady of the Rocks," comes to a culmination here.

The passage in lines 346-358 indicates an intense agony for water, thus an intense agony for baptism and salvation on the symbolic level. At line 359 "the third who walks beside you" is explained by Eliot in his note, but the suggestion is much richer than Eliot implies. Here, the Fisher King, The Man with Three Staves (from the Tarot Pack), the Hanged God of Fraser's *Golden Bough,* the Hanged Man of the fortune, and the Christ all come together into one visionary figure. The hooded figure is the resurrected Christ of Luke XXIV:15-16: "And it came to pass, that, while they communed together and reasoned, Jesus himself drew near, and went with them. But their eyes were holden that they should not know him." The passage is also reminiscent of a similar one in Walt Whitman's "When Lilacs Last in the Door-Yard Bloom'd":

> Then with the knowledge of death as walking one side of me,
> And the thought of death close-walking the other side of me,
> And I in the middle as with companions, and as holding the
>   hands of companions,
> I fled forth to the hiding receiving night that talks not,

Down to the shores of the water, the path by the swamp in the
    dimness,
To the solemn shadowy cedars and ghostly pines so still.

And the singer so shy to the rest receiv'd me,
The grey-brown bird I know receiv'd us comrades three.
And he sang the carol of death...

Perhaps the line "I do not know whether a man or a woman" ties the
hooded figure to Tiresias as well.

Lines 366-76, Eliot explains in his note, are a vision of the chaos of
eastern Europe. The vision borrows elements of horror and fear from the
tradition of the Chapel Perilous. These distorted images of chaos are in a
number of instances intentional echoes of earlier lines in the poem; thus,
the "violet air" recalls "violet hours" from section III, the "whispered
music" is reminiscent of the "whispers" in section IV, the "tolling bells
that kept the hours" evokes the reference to Saint Mary Woolnoth in line
67. The tolling bells are also associated with the Chapel Perilous, and the
hair imagery with sanctified harlotry. The word "Unreal" recalls lines 60
and 207 and the original source. In this series of chaotic images, real time
has ceased to exist. The impression is reenforced by the whole phantasmagoria of horror in the vision. It is further reenforced by the last line of
this passage, 384, which echoes "the voices of the children, singing in the
cupola," line 202.

The "decayed hole among the mountains" returns to the Chapel
Perilous. The horrors of the preceding vision are also the horrors on the
approach to the Chapel Perilous. Traditionally, in the Grail legends, the
Chapel Perilous stands in the middle of a Perilous Cemetery. The cemetery
is also full of horrors. It is suggested here by the "dry bones" which can do
no harm. The initiation ceremonies involved in the visit to the Chapel
Perilous are parallel to more ancient descents into the world of the dead.
According to Carl Jung, the important psychologist, such tales are archetypal images of the same psychological processes. In psychological terms,
there is always the grave danger that the psyche may not return to the world
of men, but may perish in the desert of the drought or pass permanently
into the realms of phantasmagoria. The Chapel Perilous is surrounded by
a Perilous Cemetery to accommodate those who have failed on the quest.
The dry bones are the bones of those who have failed, but now they are
harmless.

In the Grail legends, the passage through the Chapel Perilous indicated
that the knight was ready for the final adventure, the relieving of the Fisher

King and the subsequent breaking of the drought. Here, with the French-nursery-rhyme crowing of a cock, the drought is broken, and the rain comes. This whole section is a movement away from the waters of Leman in search of the River of Life, the holy river, the Ganges.

In a return now to the voice of the Thunder, in fact in the words of the Thunder (Datta — Give; Dayadhvam — Sympathize; Damyata — Control), derived from the Brihadaranyaka-Upanishad, the solution is given. The "DA" which alliterates with the sacred words and precedes them provides an onomatopoetic representation of the voice of the thunder. The three commandments of the thunder have been violated in the waste land. These three sections take the form of ritual response. The first antiphonally cries "Datta" (Give) — "What have we given?" and then the reply — the giving has been a surrender to passion but not to love. The protagonist enters the whirlpool as section IV has prescribed. The "real" is asserted as an act outside the life-death cycle — an act of life in the temporal pattern. Line 407 is a reference to Webster's *White Devil,* forming a link to the end of the first section of the poem.

The second antiphonal response demands "Sympathize." The "door" is the door of the prison of self in which each man is locked by his pride. Line 411 refers to a passage in Dante's *Inferno* recounting the story of Count Ugolino and his crime. The specific lines are: "I heard below the gate swung to and locked/ Beneath the dreadful tower..." As Eliot points out in his note, the passage is also indebted to F. H. Bradley's *Appearance and Reality,* which describes the prison of self as "a circle on the outside."

The third and last antiphonal response demands "Control." The passage is an "aethereal rumor" of release from sterility. The image is of a boat on a calm sea in the control of skilled hands. The boat is equated with the heart, and the response of the heart counters the surrender of the blood. Had the surrender been complete, then the heart and the boat might have been totally equated. The sailor imagery is a vague echo of the Phoenician sailor and of death by water, but also of baptism and rebirth.

The last ten lines of the poem are almost all allusions. They are the broken fragments of truth left standing in the waste land, and the speaker "shored [them] against my ruins." The first of these lines is an obvious reference to the Fisher King. The line is reminiscent of a similar line in section III: "I was fishing in the dull canal...behind the gashouse..." The Fisher King asks "Shall I at least set my lands in order?" That is, can he attempt to rebuild his ruins, to abnegate the attitude of passive negation, to do something more than sit and fish while "London Bridge is falling down."

Here follow three fragments. The protagonist says these are the fragments he has shored against his ruins. This line is followed by two references from Thomas Kyd's *Spanish Tragedy* (1592). Hieronymo has been asked to provide a "show" for the entertainment of the king. He replies that he has ready a tragedy which he wrote in his youth. He plans to use this plot, fitting the actors to the parts he wants them to play in real life, and thus execute revenge for his son's death. A strange aspect of the play, however, is that: "Each of us must act his part/ In unknown languages..." The fragments here are in foreign languages.

The first of these is related to the story of Arnaut Daniel, the Provencal poet whom Dante meets in Purgatory. He explains to Dante how he is suffering for his lustful life on earth, but how he welcomes the pain, how he sings as he weeps, because he hopes for final redemption. "Then he dived back into the fire which refines them." The second fragment is from *Pervigilium Veneris,* a song of Spring and of fulfillment. The nightingale sings, her cruel memories forgotten, and the poet alone is sad and silent. "When shall I be as the swallow, that I may cease to be voiceless." Philomela's sister Procne was turned into a swallow when Philomela was turned into a nightingale. But Eliot leaves off the end of the original line and instead repeats the word "swallow," for he wants to call attention to the nightingale and swallow images which serve as a link to the earlier references to Philomela in this poem. The last fragment is from a sonnet by Gerard de Nerval, "The Disinherited One." The poet, bereft and inconsolable, like "the Prince of Aquitaine at the truined tower," has lost all, but he hopes to rebuild his heritage. The line from Kyd's play evokes a strong recollection of *Hamlet*. The players scene in *Hamlet* employs the same plot device that Kyd used, and there are striking similarities between the characters of Hieronymo and Hamlet.

The poem closes with a repetition of the ritual words from the Upanishad and with the formal closing chant of the Upanishad—"Shantih." The word, as Eliot explains in his note, means "the Peace that Passeth Understanding." The peace that passeth understanding is attainable through rebirth, and rebirth can be achieved only through death. The waste land has been traversed, the initiation successfully endured, and baptism through both fire and water ensures the rebirth which is salvation and annihilation simultaneously.

The Waste Land has what might be called a symphonic structure; that is, it is composed of five movements which are linked by the contrapuntal interweaving of a series of recurrent themes. The themes are drawn from the Fisher King myths. The contrapuntal themes which interlace the structure are derived from centuries of general and personal experience in changeless patterns. The very number of cultures and languages and of associations with the experiences of other writers which Eliot has absorbed into the structure of his poem suggest the universality both of the theme and of the pattern. Eliot's use of quotation, allusion, and adaptation serve two essential purposes in this poem. On the one hand they illustrate the "sense of the past" which was so important an idea in Eliot's critical theories. The sense of the past "involves a perception, not only of the pastness of the past, but of its presence." On the other hand, they illustrate the tradition. In Eliot's view, a writer is compelled "to write not merely with his own generation in his bones, but with a feeling that the whole of the literature of Europe from Homer and within it the whole literature of his own country has a simultaneous existence and composes a simultaneous order."

The verse patterns of the poem follow essentially the same basic structure as the thematic patterns. Again in symphonic style, the verse varies from section to section, providing different rhythms for different functions. The verse forms in *The Waste Land* are still essentially traditional. They can be scanned as can most earlier English verse. But Eliot's theory of versification, even in this early poem, is important to note. In *The Use of Poetry,* he wrote:

> The feeling for syllable and rhythm, penetrating far below the conscious levels of thought and feeling, invigorating every work; sinking to the most primitive and forgotten, returning to the origin and bringing something back, seeking the beginning and the end. It works through meanings, certainly, or not without meanings in the ordinary sense, and fuses the old and the trite, the current, and the new and surprising, the most ancient and the most civilized mentality.

Later, in the *Four Quartets,* he was able to achieve a control of verse forms which permitted a music and a contrapuntal effect not yet possible in *The Waste Land.* But already in this poem he was experimenting with the "music" of spoken language, and the "pub scene" in section II is a beautiful demonstration of what he was able to achieve by way of shaping ordinary speech to musical patterns. More will be said about his later achievements in verse in conjunction with the discussion of the *Four Quartets.*

The time structure of the poem, however, may well be the most significant key to its understanding. The intricate and complex movement within time is achieved by the constant use of citation, allusion, reference, and adaptation. Each reference to some thing outside the poem brings into play a whole spectrum of associations connected with the thing referred to and forces the reader to bring these extraneous associations to bear on what is being said in this poem. Further, the dissolution of normal time within the poem contributes to the curious effect. "Real" time, chronological time, mathematical time, exist outside the poem, largely in terms of the duration of the readers involvement with the poem. Within the poem, time is dissolved much as space is dissolved in modern art and much as the contemporary artist Salvador Dali indicates the dissolution of time in his painting by showing clocks to be fluid. St. Augustine long ago advanced a philosophical theory of time based upon a conception of instantaneous experience. What happens, happens now, he argued; that is, a "happening" is always an experience, idea, or thing which is "present." Nevertheless, a meaningful temporal series can be constructed. "Past" means the present memory experience of a thing past; "future" means the present expectation or anticipation of a thing future.

While it is perhaps misleading to jump more than a thousand years, Henri Bergson's theory also plays an important part in Eliot's conception of time. Bergson recognized that scentific time does not endure, but rather that it attempts to eliminate duration. This recognition led him to formulate a concept of time as an immediate datum of consciousness apparent to a given human being. For Eliot, the notion of mathematical time is an abstraction. Eliot is concerned with human time in which past and present coexist in a continuum of now. *The Waste Land* dissolves mathematical time and links a universalized complex of ideas derived from the whole scope of western civilization and literature into an immediate datum of the experience of a single protagonist and transpiring in the mind of that individual in a matter of hours. Thousands of years are telescoped into a single coherent thought flashing at supersonic speed through the intelligence of one well-informed man.

The poem is an extremely complex structure, interweaving a great mass of ideas into a single relatively brief statement. Explications of the poem are often much longer than the poem, because the poem achieves its interrelations by free association, while the explication has to try to verbalize all the associations. Every reader will bring to the poem a slightly different series of experiences and will carry away from the poem a relatively different set of responses. The student should not be surprised or disappointed if his awareness of the poem is different or appears smaller than someone elses. A poem, after all, is not exactly a concrete denotative statement. It is written to appeal to the senses as well as to the logical intelligence. While its statement to the logical intelligence is paraphrasable, its statement to the senses is highly subjective for each individual recipient.

NOTES ON FIVE FAMOUS POEMS

The two poems so far discussed are the ones most commonly included in anthologies and most commonly studied. Eliot has of course written a great many other poems. This section will take up five of his best known poems. In no sense are these to be considered "minor" poems; on the contrary, *The Four Quartets* probably constitute the most important single work of Eliot's whole career. The other poems, though one or two of them are relatively brief, are also important works in themselves.

THE HOLLOW MEN

It is most logical to take up *The Hollow Men* (1925) after *The Waste Land* because it is the most nearly related to *The Waste Land*. Grover Smith, probably the most careful of Eliot's critics, maintains that most of *The Hollow Men* is made up out of the lines Ezra Pound deleted from *The Waste Land*. The poem certainly bears a strong thematic resemblance to the waste land theme.

The two epigrams, respectively out of British tradition and out of Joseph Conrad's novel, *Heart of Darkness,* point up the analogies at the center of the poem. Both Guy Fawkes and Kurtz are "lost violent souls" remembered now only as "the hollow men...the stuffed men." In Conrad's novel, Marlow, the narrator, calls Kurtz "hollow at the core." Children carry about stuffed effigies of Guy Fawkes when they solicit "a penny for the Old Guy."

The use of straw-stuffed effigies is reported by Sir James Fraser as being identified with fall rituals celebrating the death of the fertility god or Fisher King. Part I of the poem specifically depicts the scarecrow effigies of hollow men in the modern waste land. The dryness, aridness, of the waste land is certainly apparent in the first lines.

The *eyes* introduced in Part I and continued in Part II have their origin in Vergil's *Aeneid* and in Dante. In one sense they are the burning eyes of Charon, the boatman who ferries lost souls into Hades; in another context, they are the eyes of Beatrice in *Purgatorio*. On still another level they derive from the burning eyes of the mad Kurtz in Conrad's book. The speaker in this poem, which is still another dramatic monologue, is one of the hollow men. Like the other hollow men, he is waiting for the consuming fire. He has come to this condition because he has refused to see, and he shares his blindness with Tiresias.

The first four lines of Part V parody the "Mulberry Bush" chant of children, but they also evoke the Maypole ritual with its fertility connotations. The prickly pear has been substituted for its sterility, its "waste land" connotation. Other lines in the section repeat snatches of church liturgy. This poem, like *The Waste Land* and certain other poems, is about a state of mind, but unlike the other poems, there is no background or memory to account for the state. There is no "action" in a physical sense. The action is totally psychological. The poem derives much of its symbolic intensity exactly from the fact that it lacks dramatic clarity. The straw men, as represented by their spokesman, have sunk into profound misery. The poem is dominated by a sense of horror derived from a realization of earthly hell. The hollow men wait for death to liberate them from this hell into a kind of purgatory, but there is no hope of salvation even in the purgatory. The multifoliate rose of Part IV, symbol of redemption, is not accessible.

Once again, as in *The Waste Land,* there appears to be a wedding of Eastern and Western ideas. The "problem" in this poem may be stated in terms of the triumvirate of Hindu belief. Siva embodies the powers of creation and destruction as manifested in sex and in the birth-death-rebirth cycle; Brahma embodies the powers of the mind, for he is the creator of the world; Vishnu embodies the power of salvation to preserve man from evil. It is Vishnu who in his tenth incarnation will destroy the earth and reunite the divine and the created. The hollow men wait for that final destruction because between now and then there is only an endless series of birth, death, and rebirth which is inescapable and which is, in itself, a waste land not only because it is inevitable, but because it offers no salvation from the wheel on which they turn. The eyes and the rose may well be symbols like the Holy Grail; a salvation sought but unattainable. The hollow men, like the knights of the Grail legends, quest for salvation, but because they are blind, spiritually and physically, they cannot find what they seek. They are not even pure enough to pass those first initiation rites indicated in *The Waste Land.*

While it bears strong relations to *The Waste Land,* this poem does not have the complexity nor the strength of that one. Where *The Waste Land* is explicit in its statement of the problem and in its answers, this poem is ambiguous and achieves its effects through mood and tone.

JOURNEY OF THE MAGI

This poem (1927) literally recounts the story of the journey of the Magi to the birth of Christ as it is told in Matthew II:1-12. The first five lines, usually printed in quotation marks, are from a sermon preached by Lancelot Andrews, Bishop of Winchester (1555-1626). Eliot quotes the passage in his essay on "Lancelot Andrews," in *Selected Essays*. The remainder of the poem, following from this introduction, is again a dramatic monologue spoken by one of the Magi. The first half of the poem, to line 25, recounts the Biblical story, projects the inner conflict of the speaker and his colleagues, and establishes the symbolic and the natural levels of the journey. Again, the poem is concerned with a quest. Again, the questors must traverse a waste land.

On the natural level, the journey is one from death to life, from "The very dead of winter" to "a temperate valley...smelling of vegetation," from the waste land to the renewed land. The references to the Fisher King myth are obvious. With the rebirth of the savior, the land is also reborn. Thus, symbolically, the journey is from life to death; from the life of the old order, "The summer palaces on slopes, the terraces,/ And the silken girls bringing sherbet" to the symbolic death of that order signified by the line "An old white horse galloped away in the meadow."

The "running stream" and the "water-mill" have been identified as personal images for Eliot; things he once saw from a moving train [see *The Use of Poetry...*, p. 141]. But the running stream is also symbolic of time continuity; thus, the watermill beats the darkness of time, and the future is unknowable. The Magi reflect this idea when "At the end we preferred to travel all night." The first half of the poem suggests the central ambiguity of the Life-in-Death, Death-in-Life theme which is resolved in the second half of the poem.

It is not only the "voices singing in our ears" that appraise the Magi of the "folly" of their journey. The middle stanza of the poem contains a whole series of images, skillfully balanced between birth and death. The first three lines of that stanza contain birth images—dawn, temperate valley, wet, smelling of vegetation, running stream. The next five lines contain a series of images foreshadowing the Crucifixion—three trees on the low sky (the three crosses on Golgotha), hands dicing (the soldiers who threw dice for Christ's clothing), pieces of silver (with which Judas was paid).

The white horse is the central and key image in the poem. White horses have a tremendously rich mythic association. The symbol may refer to the militant Christ of Revelations (VI:2, XIX:11), or to the white horse the Vishnu will ride when he destroys the world in order to reunite the divine and the created, or to the countless identifications of Fisher King figures with white horses as in the case of Saint George. There is also a possibility, since this horse "galloped away," that the reference is intended to evoke G. K. Chesterton's *Ballad of the White Horse* in which the gradual fading away of a stone white horse represents the fading of paganism under the onslaught of Christianity. Appearing where it does in the poem, this symbol clears away "the old dispensations," and prepares the stage for the new order symbolized by the birth and foreshadowed death of Christ.

The last half of the poem is marked by understatement, an outgrowth of the failure of the speaker to understand what he has seen and to willingly give up the old dispensations. The narrator is confused, and his confusion is reflected in the strange breakup of the lines "...but set down/ This set down/ This," and in the question immediately following: "were we led all this way for/ Birth or Death?"

The poem appears to be broken into two parts; the first dealing with birth-death, the second with death-rebirth. The birth-death ambiguity which the last stanza explicitly states is incorporated into the contrasting balanced symbols at the center of the poem. Finally, the speaker knows that the death of his old beliefs will make no more difference to the world than will the death of Christ already foreshadowed by the depravity around him; that is, his personal salvation is pointless. Still, the Magi persist in their advent, undergo a symbolic death by giving up their "old dispensations," and discover at last that such a death is the only way to rebirth. At the end, therefore, they wait for a final death.

This poem belongs to a group of poems known as the "Ariel Poems" because they were published as Christmas poems, over a period of five years beginning in 1927, under that general title. The poem is thematically related to "Gerontion," but it differs from it in that it ignores the sweep of history. It is, however, the drama of a bewildered shaken man, and in that sense appears to be an accurate representation of Eliot's own internal struggle. The position in this poem constitutes a spiritual advance over that held in *The Waste Land*. It must be remembered that Eliot became an Anglican in 1927.

GERONTION

The poem (1919) is somewhat earlier than *The Waste Land*. Again, it is a monologue, this time one in which an old man reminisces about his lost power to live and his lost hope of spiritual rebirth. The pose of an old man is fairly common in Eliot's early poetry (see for example the discussion of "Prufrock"). In this poem, sterility and paralysis, waste land characteristics, are woven out of the old man's losses of faith. The technique in this poem is the stream-of-consciousness technique used so successfully later in the *The Waste Land.* One of the manifestations of the technique is the broad use of allusion, also a technique more skillfully developed in *The Waste Land.* Here, as in the later poetry, Eliot uses allusion to fulfill the historical sense of which he spoke in the essay "Tradition and the Individual Talent" (1917). The allusions in this poem are drawn largely from Elizabethan and Jacobean dramatists like Chapman, Middleton, Shakespeare, and Jonson. Eliot attempts to make the past appear to be the present. The past can be present because the memory of it presently exists. At the same time, Eliot wants to use the past to explain the contemporaneousness of the present by contrast.

The earlier section on modern poetry points out many of the devices of older poetry. In this poem, Eliot is not only indebted to the Elizabethans and Jacobeans for pertinent allusion, but he is also heavily indebted for verse forms and for rhythm. The rhythm of this poem is almost completely iambic pentameter, but it is not a rigid meter. Eliot was fascinated with the variations that the Elizabethans were able to impose upon that metrical form, and he borrows both the form and the variations *in toto.*

In terms of the stream-of-consciousness technique employed, the poem is heavily indebted to James Joyce. Some critics seem to feel that this poem was influenced by *Ulysses,* but it is more likely that *Portrait of the Artist as a Young Man* has the greatest influence, since *Ulysses* was not completely published until a year after this poem had appeared. There are scenes and passages in the two works which are startlingly similar even to their terminology. Both Stephen Dedalus and Gerontion seem to be obsessed with a concept of personal responsibility for sin, both as a personal and as an abstract phenomenon. The principal difference between the use of stream of consciousness in this poem and in *The Waste Land* lies in the fact that in this poem the emphasis in placed upon what is remembered, while *The Waste Land* stresses the act of remembering. "Gerontion" concerns remembrance, but *The Waste Land* concerns memory.

Superficially, in this poem, as in *The Waste Land,* what appears to be contrasted is the "good old days" and "the bad new days." But it is easier to see, in this poem, that if such a contrast exists, it is extremely superficial. The contrast that is important is the contrast between the secular history of western man and the promise of salvation through Christ. The history of western man is paralleled by Gerontion. The mysterious figures—Mr. Silvero, Hakagawa, Madame de Tornquist, Fraulein von Kulp—are symbols of the modern inheritors of the desolation; they are, as their names imply, international, rootless. Christ is both sweet redeemer and tiger of destruction. He comes in "Depraved May," the Easter season, the time of crucifixion and denial. Depraved May returns annually, rhythmically, in any age and in every age, whenever the life of the senses stirs without love. Spring both stirs lust and answers lust. It is the Spring which stirs the aged Gerontion into his monologue.

This poem is interesting largely as a training ground for *The Waste Land*. All of the techniques which Eliot brought to fruition in the latter poem were tested in this one. The dissolution of time, the system of allusion, and even the metrical experimentation within the limits of a much older metrical system, all were used and tested in "Gerontion." The religious ideas, derived from Augustine and St. John of the Cross, the philosophical ideas, from Bergson and Gourmont, the literary ideas, from Joyce, are all woven into the fabric of this poem, foreshadowing the more sophisticated use of all of them in *The Waste Land*.

While the poem is a prelude to *The Waste Land,* it is still a significant work in its own right. It is certainly an advance over "Prufrock," a poem in which the problem is personal so that its social applicability has to be inferred. By contrast, here the overt statements about history constitute a critique of civilization. But even so, the poem is a symbolization of a problem which the Fisher King myths in Jessie Weston's book made it possible for him to objectify in *The Waste Land*. This poem helps to point up the continuity of Eliot's thinking, for Gerontion is a Fisher King figure without the framework of the myth. There is a real kinship between Gerontion and Tiresias.

ASH WEDNESDAY

The poem (1930), like *The Waste Land* and *The Hollow Men*, appears disjointed. The occasion is the beginning of Lent, a day of weeping, fasting, and repentance for the sins of the past. On this day, Christians ask God's help to turn back toward Him and away from the temptations and evils of the world and the flesh. Proper scriptural referents include Psalms 6, 32, 38, 51, 102, 130 and 143 as well as Jonah, Isaiah 58, and Hebrews 12. These are evoked or quoted in the poem. Eliot also refers to several Ash Wesnesday sermons preached by Lancelot Andrews (see note on *Journal of the Magi).*

Like the other poems examined, this one too is a dramatic monologue. The protagonist is a man plunged into despair. He takes excursions in memory similar to those in *The Waste Land,* but this poem has a greater dramatic unity because it has a more precise temporal focus. While time is still treated in human rather than mathematical terms, the chronological sequence of the poem is more apparent. Like several of the poems discussed above, it concerns itself with the conflict between the values of the flesh and those of the spirit. The values of the flesh are given objective reality in terms of sensuous memories of a past life. The values of the spirit are stated in terms of a quest for union with The Word. The symbol of salvation is the dream woman of Part IV. While she is never identified, it is possible that she is identified on the one hand with the Virgin and on the other hand with the Beatrice of Dante's *Purgatorio.* In her double role, she serves to unite the divine and the human. The human aspect of the woman is identified with all phases of human love, both carnal and spiritual, while the spiritual aspect is identified with the divine because she has access to The Word. The human woman perhaps has been an object of desire. In Part I, the protagonist is deprived of her presence and thus finds himself unable to turn toward her. Symbolically, he is cut off from love, both human and divine. He has long ago renounced sexual love.

The middle of the poem consists of four parts, each devoted to a particular aspect of mystical enlightenment. The theology of the poem is drawn largely from *The Ascent of Mt. Carmel* and the unfinished *Dark Night of the Soul,* both written by St. John of the Cross. It is the dark night with which the poem is concerned; the advance of the soul toward God and perfection by a process of negating desire. The four middle parts of the poem reflect the stages of the active and passive progress of the soul. The first of these shows the rejection of carnal love; the second proves the persistence of desire; the third illustrates the lost vision of light (a Tiresian blindness), and the fourth demonstrates the inability of human weakness to attain The Word. The last section of the poem is a prayer to the Virgin for intercession and for grace. The poem demonstrated Eliot's view of love as simultaneously a spiritual and a human power.

A significant difference between this poem and *The Waste Land* lies in the fact that the woman here is no longer merely a fertility symbol. A human woman in this poem has been raised to a spiritual level on which her sexuality has become blended with her spirituality. In *The Waste Land,* once the symbol for sexuality has been put aside, the quest for the Grail goes on without it, but here the woman becomes a symbol of more than sexuality, and a reunion with her becomes actually a step forward in the process of achieving·union with The Word. The poem may, in this sense, be regarded as an allegory of man's relation to the church.

The protagonist in this poem shares with Tiresias and with the hollow men a similar despair, but he is somewhat advanced over them, for the poem begins showing him to have a knowledge which the others acquire only at the end of their quests; that the quest for salvation requires discipline transcending mere denial of carnal love. That quest may require the loss of spiritual certainty. Here the protagonist waits patiently until the separation is ended; he wants only to endure.

> Because I cannot hope to turn again
> Consequently I rejoice, having to construct something
> Upon which to rejoice.

The metrical scheme of this poem is still traditional in every sense. This poem cannot be considered among Eliot's best work. He seems to have allowed his plot to grow out of the allusions to other works rather than to govern the allusions in terms of the plot. The poem also seems needlessly wordy and involved. Some critics have accused Eliot of willful mystification. Nevertheless, like many of the poems discussed, this one has an effect which derives out of the texture of tone and imagery alone, which is not dependent upon the "message." It may be said, however, that the amount of research required by the context of the poem is not justified by amount of reward the poem has to offer. It is not philosophically, nor theologically, nor technically original, but it is extremely difficult.

THE FOUR QUARTETS

The Four Quartets (1943) marks Eliot's most mature and most advanced poetry. It is, as Helen Gardner has remarked, Eliot's "masterpiece...[containing] more fully than any of his earlier works the poetic solution of his peculiar problems as a poet..." His *Waste Land* period appears to end definitely with the publication in 1932 of the second part of *Coriolan*. Between that time and the publication of the *Quartets,* Eliot made a protracted visit to the United States, and he took a long break from lyric poetry during the years when he concerned himself principally with dramatic material. During the interval, he published five brief poems jointly called *Landscapes* in which he experimented with the new forms and new ideas fully developed in the *Quartets*.

The structure of the *Quartets* is enormously complex. First, the quartets have a symphonic structure in which each represents a sonata form composed in turn of specific movements. Each of the voices in the poem represents an orchestral instrument. The general music is the music of speech, but he has discovered how to vary the music of speech so that the range from the colloquial to the formal in terms of diction is broader than ever attempted by him before. Second, the poem contains musical bridges between the instrumental passages; thus, the technique consists of a passage of exposition of theme, a passage of development of theme, a passage of recapitulation, a bridge, and then a repetition of the pattern. Third, there is in the poem a contrapuntal arrangement of subject matter corresponding with the musical structure of the verse. The central theme of this poem concerns the union of the constant change of time with the absolute stillness of eternity. This theme is an obvious outgrowth of Eliot's concern with the contrast between real and ideal, between human and spiritual in his earlier poetry. Once again, philosophical considerations of time are extremely significant in the structure of the poem.

The four part structure carries through on a variety of levels. Some critics see in the poem a reflection of the fourfold structure of Dante's *Divine Comedy* — literal, allegorical, moral, and mystical levels. The themes of the poem are also fourfold — they are history, poetry, love, and faith. Their interaction on the temporal level points to a transfiguration on the eternal level. Furthermore, each of the sections corresponds to a season of the year and to one of the "basic elements," earth, water, air, and fire. These maintain the cycle of change in time against which Eliot places the idea of a stable, still eternity. The poem also recalls the birth-death-rebirth cycle which Eliot so effectively employed in his earlier poetry, but while the wounded god, the Fisher King, the quest, and the purgation by fire are still here, they are now in the background rather than at the center. The *Quartets* are characterized by a philosophical and emotional calm quite in contrast to the despair and suffering of the earlier works.

The names of the sections come from place names which had personal significance for Eliot. Burnt Norton is a country house in Gloucestershire where Eliot stayed in the summer of 1934; East Coker is a village in Somersetshire from which the Eliot family originated; Dry Salvages are a group of rocks off Cape May which Eliot remembered from his childhood, and Little Gidding was the original location of an Anglican community, established in 1625, which Eliot visited in 1936.

Perhaps one of the most important contributions of the *Quartets*, however, lies in the area of metrics. The music of the *Quartets* goes beyond denoting speech alone; it implies the sound and rhythm of spoken words, but it also signifies the structure of interrelationships among different kinds of speech and other poetic materials. The extent ranges from the colloquial to the oratorical. The verse form which constitutes the base for this poem is the four-stress line with strong medial pauses. This is quite a departure from the existing traditions of English verse. Eliot rediscovered the value of the alliterated four-stress line of medieval English, but he was able to use it with a flexibility which overcame its inherent monotony and rigidity. The first section of the *Quartets* opens with an excellent example:

> ´   ´   ´   ´
> Time present / and time past
> ´   ´   ´   ´
> Are both perhaps present / in time future
> ´   ´   ´   ´
> And ti. e future / contained in time past.

This passage indica. s the base line as well as three-stress and five-stress variations of the line. In this kind of verse, alliteration is significant. Note the repetition of /t/ sounds in *time, future,* and *contained,* and the repetition of /p/ in *present, past,* and *perhaps.* In this kind of verse, only the primary stresses are counted, and the number of weak stresses which occur between the primary stresses does not matter. For example, in the first line, there are three weak stresses between the first and second strong stresses and no weak stresses between the second and third strong stresses.

The three-stress line serves frequently to bridge other sections. The closing passage of the first section, leading into the second section is such a passage:

> ´   ´   ´
> Sudden in a shaft of sunlight
> ´   ´   ´
> Even while the dust moves...

Another common variation is the six-stress line, which is really a doubling of the three-stress line. The opening passage of the second movement illustrates the point:

> ´ ´   ´   ´
> At the stillpoint of the turning world./ Neither
> ´   ´
> flesh nor fleshless
> ´   ´   ´   ´
> Neither from nor towards;/ at the still point,
> ´   ´   ´
> there the dance is...

There are, of course, special sections in which special rhythmical effects are employed, like the "canto" section in *Little Gidding* in which Eliot attempted to achieve the "nearest equivalent to a canto of the Inferno or Purgatorio." As he points out himself, the versification is a modified terza rima lacking rhyme, but the overall effect is very close to blank verse.

Eliot's experimentation in the writing of dramatic verse led him to the creation of the meter he has employed for non-dramatic purposes in the *Quartets,* a poem which certainly marks the mature achievement of a poet who had long experimented with the English language. This new verse is really a return to Middle English accentual meter, but it contains greater freedom within the line thereby eliminating the monotony of the older, more rigid line.

The verse form which Eliot "invented" for the *Quartets* has had a most profound effect on his followers and his contemporaries. The twentieth century has been marked by a vast variety of experiments in metrical form. Probably none have been so widely accepted as Eliot's. This is not to imply that others have not been as important in liberating modern verse from the limitations of convention. Some perhaps have been more important, but Eliot has been the poet of the century who has had the widest audience, both academic and popular, and his influence has been more widespread than that of any other poet of this century. In addition to his influence as a metricist, his ideas and his spiritual voyage seem to have been common to the age.

INTRODUCTION TO DRAMA

Verse drama reached its most popular and its most highly developed form during the Renaissance. Although some verse drama has been written since that time, little of it has had any lasting significance on the stage. In the Eighteenth century, Dryden and others continued to write verse drama which was acted upon the stage, but the form of the heroic couplet, commonly employed by Eighteenth century writers, tended to make the form stilted. During the Eighteenth century, the ballad opera became a fairly popular form, and verse drama moved more and more in the direction of musical comedy and light theater. During the Nineteenth century, poets like Tennyson attempted to write serious verse dramas, but for the most part these were closet dramas; that is, they were rarely or never acted on the stage. In the early Twentieth century verse drama was "rediscovered," as is apparent through the tremendous number of Shakespearean companies performing throughout the United States and England every summer. As the century wore on, other writers took up the form. Sherwood Anderson and Christopher Fry appear to have had the broadest success, although others have employed the form.

T. S. Eliot was one of the most important of the verse dramatists of the period. His career as a dramatist divides his productive life into three periods; the *Waste Land* period, from 1917 to 1932; the dramatic period, from 1932 to 1943; and the final period, from 1943 to his death in 1965. The dramatic period provided an apprenticeship in versification which took Eliot out of the conventional forms he had employed during the *Waste Land* period and perpared him for the verse experiments and the achievement of the *Four Quartets*.

By 1933, in *The Use of Poetry*, Eliot was remarking that "the ideal medium for poetry...is the theatre." By 1936 he had come to the conclusion that poetry was "the natural and complete medium for the drama." He felt that poetry provided, under the action, the advantage of a pattern of music which could intensify the viewer's excitement through a reinforcement from the deeper level derived out of song and incantation. With this idea in mind, he carefully sought to recreate in the verse of his drama, the incantatory rhythms of liturgy, but with a modern vocabulary and a cadence common to ordinary speech.

In "The Rock," (1934) Eliot mixed seven or eight different types of verse, ranging from the effects of comic song, derived from Kipling, through imitation of clumsy and unmusical free verse in the lines ascribed to the Redshirts, through a regular, heavy, footstamping, jazzy beat in the lines of the Blackshirts, to the Swinburnean lyricism of the final chorus. In general, in this play, the verse is still iambic pentameter, but this meter gives way repeatedly, in passages of excitement or incantation, to a poetic prose having highly irregular stress patterns and a fairly large number of anapestic substitutions.

In *Murder in the Cathedral* (1935) the verse is not so miscellaneous, and this tends to give the play a greater structural unity. Eliot has said that he had in mind the versification of *Everyman*, a 15th century morality play of Dutch origin, written in English in a medieval accentual verse form. The play, and particularly the Tempters' dialogues with Becket, are marked by the sharp, irregularly assorted stresses, four to a line, which closely mimic the medieval predecessor. To some extent, Eliot even introduces alliteration into the verse.

Basically, with small variation, this verse form constitutes the metrical base for both *The Family Reunion* and *The Cocktail Party*, although in these plays the verse appears to be more artificial than it was in *Murder in the Cathedral*. Even Eliot was aware of this deficiency, for he once remarked that the verse in *The Family Reunion* seemed to him to be "remote from the necessity of Action."

Verse drama is an exceedingly difficult form to write, because reality is often at odds with the limitations of verse form. The drama strives normally for a certain amount of verisimilitude to life. If the characters do not speak and react according to the dictates of reality, the viewer is likely to lose the drama in the language. In order for verse drama to be successful, the verse must be written in such a way that on the one hand it is believable as dialogue while at the same time on the other hand it conforms to the rigid requirements of verse form. If the language loses the rigidity of verse patterns, then it is no longer verse, or at least it is no longer successful verse. On the contrary, no matter how good the verse is, if the dialogue is not believable as dialogue, the play loses its validity as drama. The genius of Shakespeare lies in his ability to use blank verse, unrhymed iambic pentameter lines, to create a dialogue which sounds as though it might have been spoken by a living human being. Relatively few dramatists have been able to accomplish this effect. The failure of most Eighteenth century drama may be traced in part at least to a defect in the verse. The extreme rigidity of the heroic couplet does not allow the flexibility in line structure which is necessary to a believable dialogue. The failure of most closet drama also exemplifies this problem. Closet drama is often fine verse but unactable drama because while the ideas are interesting, the dramatic effects of interaction between characters are hampered by the very excellence of the verse.

Another fact must be taken into consideration. In theatrical terms, some acts are pretty tough to follow. After Milton's *Paradise Lost* no one has seriously attempted to write an epic in English, because Milton had wrung from the form all that it had to give. After Shakespeare, very little new is left for other writers. While verse dramas have been written in English since the high point of the Renaissance, no one has been able to approach the effects that Shakespeare seemed to achieve with such ease. Anyone writing verse drama today must realize that his product will be compared with Shakespeare's, and that only a work of genius will be able to compete to any degree. One must admire anyone who attempts to write verse drama today for sheer courage if nothing else. Eliot's verse drama, while it does not approach Shakespeare's, is certainly creditable.

It is exactly because the verse form itself is so vastly important in the evaluation of any verse drama that the section of Modern Poetry has been included and that some discussion of verse form in the various plays by Eliot has been inserted into this section. Eliot's major achievement in verse drama has been the creation of a verse form in the modern idiom which is capable of being both verse and believable dialogue at the same time. While Eliot's drama is interesting in its own right, the major reason for its inclusion in these Notes consists in its transitional importance between Eliot's verse of the *Waste Land* period and his verse in the *Four Quartets*. It was the experience of writing for the stage and of trying to create a verse form that would be believable as dialogue that enabled Eliot to devise the form which dominates the *Quartets* and which may constitute his most important single contribution to modern verse and to the growth of Anglo-American literature. In general, the same kinds of themes are explored in the drama that have already been explored in the verse. As drama, these plays are not likely to have an important or lasting effect on the history or development of the theater.

MURDER IN THE CATHEDRAL

Murder in the Cathedral was written for the Canterbury Festival of June 1935. There are six separate and different published versions of this play: the abbreviated version of 1935, the complete version of 1935, revisions in 1936, 1937, and 1938, and a film version printed in 1952. The second edition, issued in the United States in 1936, is probably the best of these, since some of the others omit certain speeches, reassign others, and generally simplify the knights' speeches and the sermon. Only the film version adds entirely new material, namely a preliminary speech spoken by Becket to the Ecclesiastics of Canterbury, several new speeches for the chorus, a prose trial scene in which Becket confronts King Henry, an address by the Prior to the people of Canterbury delivered in front of the Cathedral, and a total revision of the knights' prose speeches at the end of the play. These Notes are based upon the second edition, 1936, but in general the remarks are applicable to any of the versions except the film script.

The basic plot concerns the death and martyrdom of Thomas à Becket. Thomas was born probably in 1118, the son of a Norman aristocratic family. He was educated in London and Paris where he received degrees in Canon Law. He became the personal friend and confidant of Henry II who subsequently appointed him Chancellor of England. Throughout his early career, Thomas was known as a high living fellow completely devoted to the every whim of his royal friend. In 1162, Henry II, involved in a battle with the clergy over the question of whether the King had legal authority over clergy, appointed Thomas Archbishop of

Canterbury in the mistaken conviction that Thomas would continue his loyalty to the King. Thomas accepted the post reluctantly. Once he became Archbishop, Thomas reversed his position and opposed the king's measures against the special privileges of the clergy. The struggle between Henry and Thomas was a long and bitter one, and Thomas was finally forced into exile. He lived in Europe for seven years. Because a reconciliation with the king had been effected, he returned to England, but the peace was of short duration. The king, in a fit of anger, made use of hasty words which led four knights to murder Becket in the false assumption that they were acting in accord with the King's wishes. Thomas was murdered in his own cathedral on December 29, 1170. It is said that he met his death with splendid courage. His grave became the most famous shrine in Christendom, and Henry himself did penance there. Thomas was canonized in 1173, and his official festival is observed on July 7th.

The story of Becket's life would seem to hold great dramatic and tragic potentialities. The horrible deed which culminated his life involves persons who, though not directly related by blood ties, were certainly bound by old ties of friendship and honor. Furthermore, the deed has a peculiar horror contributed to it by the addition of sacrilege to murder. While the conflict of church and state is implicit in the play, it is kept in the background. Eliot also carefully avoided the drama of personal conflict; so carefully, in fact, that Henry does not even appear in the play. The knights who perform the murder are not persons; rather, at first they are a mob, and later they are a personified set of attitudes. In the play, they lack any sort of personal motives or personal passions.

The central theme of the play is martyrdom in the strictest, oldest sense of the word. In this sense, the martyr is not the sufferer, but rather the witness to the awesome reality of the supernatural. The murder of Thomas is, in this play, and on one level, unimportant. Certainly it is not important as a dramatic climax toward which all that has happened earlier inevitably leads. Eliot himself has several times stated that the sequence of events in the play lacks the normal dramatic logic of motive-act-result. This sequence of events depends exclusively upon the will of God. Becket says so in the speech that serves as a bridge for the entrance of the Tempters:

> For a little time the hungry hawk
> Will only soar and hover, circling lower,
> Waiting excuse, pretence, opportunity.
> End will be simple, sudden, God-given.

But in the long scene which follows, Thomas can hardly be said to be tempted. The play opens so near its dramatic climax, temporally speaking, that any inner development in Thomas is quite impossible. In fact, except for the last temptation, the Tempters provide little more than a recapitulation of what has already ceased to tempt. They do not represent a present trial, and that is why Thomas can so easily dismiss them. The last temptation is so subtle that is is really impossible to judge whether or not Thomas succumbs to it. Though Thomas actually says, at the conclusion of the scene, "Now is the way clear, now is the meaning plain:/ Temptation shall not come in this kind again," a question has been raised that cannot be answered dramatically and that must, in terms of the play, simply be set aside. It may be assumed that Thomas dies with a pure will.

The second act of the play, following the interlude, has no strife at all. The martyr's sermon, which constitutes the interlude, flatly states that "a martyrdom is never the design of man," that martyrdom cannot be "the effect of a man's will to become a saint." Thomas has only to await the action. When the knights rush in, the momentary drama and shock of their eruption breaks against the static calm of Thomas, and the murder itself takes place as a kind of ritual slaughter of an unresisting victim; a necessary act, not in itself exciting or significant.

In most of his serious work, Eliot has been concerned with the quest for vision and the despair of attaining it. This quest has been pointed out in various contexts in the Notes concerning every poem included in this book. In *Murder in the Cathedral*, Thomas à Becket, the protagonist, seeks a way to live up to his great mission, martyrdom, by divorcing his awareness of it from his own ambition for fame and for canonization. But, in terms of the play, Thomas is less a man than the embodiment of an attitude. There is, in the play, a contempt for personality and its expression through acts. Normally, in an effective dramatic situation, the protagonist of a play must be conscious and aware of what is happening to him. That is, by definition, part of his function as protagonist. It is through him that the situation is made clear to the audience and often to the other characters as well. It is in him that the implications of the drama which are hidden from the other persons involved in the action are revealed. But if there is no action, in the normal sense of the word, if the center of the play is a state of mind, then the protagonist can be only self-aware. That is exactly the situation in *Murder in the Cathedral*. Thomas is only self-aware, but in terms of what Eliot is attempting to accomplish, that is adequate to the "message" of the play. Whether or not it is sufficient to the drama of the play is another question.

To put it in another way, in *Murder in the Cathedral*, the focus of interest is egocentric. The hero's character is not analyzed, as it is in *Hamlet;* in fact, the hero's character is irrelevant. Instead, the hero's martyrdom is analyzed. And it is analyzed not to show how it was actuated by a positive love of God and man, but rather to show how Thomas resisted the temptation to be martyred for the wrong reason. The wrong reason, obviously, is spiritual pride.

The chorus, which represents ordinary people, the people of Canterbury, consists of onlookers, of persons who are only passively concerned with the futility of time and change. Thomas is not related to them in any way; he is isolated from the community. His isolation is in part the result of the fact that they cannot understand what is happening to him except in the most obvious sense. That he is in some physical danger is apparent even to them, but the idea that he might be on the verge of martyrdom, or even of death, is an idea which has no reality for them. They are of a different order than he is. In one sense, of course, he is an aristocrat and they are ordinary, but in quite another sense he is spiritually prepared for his experience, and they, not having renounced carnality, are in no sense prepared even to witness, let alone to participate. Thus, under these circumstances Thomas' superiority can be expounded only to himself. The other characters in the drama—the priests, the tempters, and even the knights, are really extension, not of the personality of Thomas, but rather of the idea of which he is the personification.

In spite of these deficiencies, *Murder in the Cathedral* is a successful play of enormous emotional power. For all its lack of action and its unconvincing protagonist, the play is intensely moving. The real drama of the play is to be found, in fact, where its greatest poetry lies—in the choruses. The change which is the nature of drama is there; from the terror of the supernatural expressed at the opening of the play—"Some presage of an act/ Which our eyes are compelled to witness, has compelled our feet/ Towards the cathedral..."—to the rapturous recognition of the "glory displayed in all creatures of the earth." The fluctuations of the chorus, temporal changes which reflect the theme, are the real measure of Thomas' spiritual conquest. While Thomas is the chief protagonist in the drama, perhaps the chorus is the hero of the drama, but an unconventional hero— one who does not physically participate in the action, one who is only an observer isolated from the action.

Murder in the Cathedral is most like *Ash Wednesday* in its choice of a Christian theme, in its employment of liturgical material, and in its contrasts between the ideal of sanctity and the reality of the common experience of ordinary unsanctified humanity. The problems that the play poses are very similar to the problems posed in the poem, and the solution offered in the play is also similar to the one offered in the poem. It is a negative mysticism which permits Thomas to be martyred for the right reason. The solution is most clearly expressed in the closing chorus:

>...Thy glory is declared even in that which denies
>Thee; the darkness declares the glory of light.
>Those who deny Thee could not deny Thee, if Thou didst
>not exist; and their denial is never complete,
>for if it were so, they would not exist...

Indeed, as Eliot has shown in *Ash Wednesday,* the quest for salvation may require as a discipline the loss of spiritual certainty.

In his essays lamenting the separation of poetry and drama, Eliot has suggested the creation of a new form wedding the two. Since drama must be popular, he suggested a development of some popular technique like that of the music hall. In *Sweeney Agonistes* he employed devices drawn from the classic Greek theater and filtered through the music hall. But in *Murder in the Cathedral* he went even further. Here he unites good poetry and good theater, using the chorus of the classic Greek drama, and the sense of doom traditionally ascribed to the function of that chorus, linked with the Tempters, whose ancestry lies in the medieval morality play, and the enlarged peephole chamber, derived from the nineteenth century realistic theater of Henrik Ibsen. For the key structural device, however, Eliot has returned to the most primitive form of tragedy. His model is drawn from the earliest plays of Aeschylus.

Although *Murder in the Cathedral* does not provide the experience of an ordinary play, the experience is a dramatic one. The identification of the audience is with the chorus, and through that identification the audience becomes not a group of completely passive spectators, but rather a group which shares in the mystery although, like the chorus, it may not completely understand that mystery. The play transcends its origins, and the chorus becomes humanity confronted with the mysteries of holiness and iniquity. The audience, identified with the chorus, may not understand the man who allows himself to become a martyr, for whatever reason, but they share in the experience of seeing it happen, "right before your very eyes" as the pitchmen say.

While the experience of the play is a moving one, there are some problems connected with the play. Like several of his other plays, *Murder in the Cathedral* is full of dramatic moments and dramatic poetry. But dramatic incident and dramatic verse do not add up to drama. The problem with this play, as with others he has written, lies in the question of whether or not the central subject has been dramatically conceived, and further whether or not that central subject is capable of dramatic treatment at all. In this case the answer seems to be a categorical "no!" The central idea of this play is philosophically conceived and as a philosophical idea, it is not really capable of dramatic treatment. All the more wonder that the play is successful, but that it is successful cannot be denied. One is faced with somewhat the same problem that one encounters in trying to analyze the novels of Charles Dickens. Dickens did everything wrong. Any critic worth his salt can point to countless technical flaws in any one of his novels. And yet the novels do succeed, as popular works and as literary master-pieces. Eliot's play is similar in that it is full of devices which should pre-vent it from being a successful drama, and yet in spite of all this, it is a successful drama. Eliot has successfully rendered his vision of the boredom (as in "Prufrock"), the horror (as in *The Waste Land*), and the glory (as in *Ash Wednesday*) of life into dramatic terms, and he has done so in what is perhaps the best dramatic verse written in English since the middle of the seventeenth century. But then, all of Eliot's best poetry is dominated by a sense of the dramatic. It has been pointed out several times in these Notes that the major poems are all dramatic monologues in which the action is psychological rather than chronological or logical. His dramas are the poems translated into dialogues.

Like all of his major work, this play contains intentionally employed echoes of other works and other writers. It also contains intentional echoes of his own work. It is worthwhile to trace certain of these through the play.

Echoes of "Prufrock" occur in the last of the speeches ascribed to the fourth Tempter:

> All things are unreal,
> Unreal or disappointing;
> The Catherine wheel, the pantomime cat,
> The prizes given at the children's party...
> All things become less real, man passes
> From unreality to unreality.

and in one of the lines given to the chorus in the second part of the play: "I have lain on the floor of the sea and breathed with the breathing of the sea-anemone..."

The Waste Land appears to be evoked in the following lines:

"...and the land became brown sharp points of death in a
waste of water and mud..."

Chorus, Part I

"What sign of the spring of the year?
Only the death of the old: not a stir, not a shoot, not a breath.
Do the days begin to lengthen?
Longer and darker the day, shorter and colder the night.
Still and stifling the air: but a wind is stored up in the East.
The starved crow sits in the field, attentive; and in the wood
The owl rehearses the hollow note of death."

Opening Chorus, Part II

"...I wander in a land of barren boughs: if I break them,
they bleed;
I wander in a land of dry stones: if I touch them they bleed."

Chorus as Becket is murdered, Part II

The *Four Quartets* are anticipated in two related speeches:

"...both are fixed
In an eternal action, an eternal patience
To which all must consent that it may be willed
And which all must suffer that they may will it,
That the pattern may subsist, for the pattern is the action
And the suffering, that the wheel may turn and still
Be forever still."

Thomas, entering speech, Part I

The words of this speech are repeated almost exactly in the last speech
of the fourth Tempter. Even the *Journey of the Magi* is echoed in the
play: "...A fear like birth and death, when we see birth and death alone/
In a void apart..." This passage occurs in a line ascribed to the chorus
in the first act.

There are, as has been noted, echoes of particular works by other
writers in this play. The Knights' combined speech, just preceding the
murder of Becket, is highly reminiscent of Vachel Lindsay's "Daniel
Jazz." Thomas' speech which comes immediately after the knights' choral
passage, opens with a line from Proverbs, 28: "It is the just man who/ Like
a bold lion, should be without fear." The passage cited above as reminiscent of *The Waste Land* — "...I wander in a land of barren boughs..." —
is also strongly reminiscent of Dante's *Inferno* and of the description of

the Underworld in Virgil's *Aeneid*. The Third Priest, in his last speech, says: "Go, weak sad men, lost erring souls, homeless in earth or heaven ..." The line is a paraphrase from Thomas Heywood's *Hercule Furens* (Eliot cites the line in his essay on Seneca). The last lines of this same speech echo *Iphigenia in Tauris*. In more general terms, the Tempters are drawn from the medieval morality play convention. The concept of the wheel, so significant here, is derived from Aristotle: "Everything is moved by pushing and pulling. Hence just as in the case of the wheel, so here there must be a point which remains at rest, and from that point the movement must originate" *(De Anima, iii, 10)*. Like *Ash Wednesday,* the play derives its philosophical and theological foundations from St. John of the Cross, from Augustine and the Christian mystics.

The metrical form, as has been noted, is strongly reminiscent of Middle English alliterative verse; so much so that passages may be cited which seem derivitive, although no specific referent has been found for them:

> Winter shall come bringing death from the sea,
> Ruinous spring shall beat at our doors,
> Root and shoot shall eat our eyes and our ears...

> We have had enough of waiting, from December to dismal
> December.
> The Archbishop shall be at our head, dispelling dismay and
> doubt.

> You should wait for trap to snap
> Having severed your turn, broken and crushed.
> As for barons, envy of lesser men
> Is still more stubborn than king's anger.
> Kings have public policy, barons private profit,
> Jealousy raging possession of the fiend.

> ...No colours, no forms to distract, to divert the soul
> From seeing itself, foully united forever, nothing with nothing,
> Nor what we call death, but what beyond death is not death,
> We fear, we fear...

It is not likely that these lines are actually allusions, since the content is quite clearly Eliot's own. Rather, his imitation of earlier verse forms is so skillful in these lines that they could well be medieval except for their content. The alliteration and the internal caesurae give the lines this appearance along with the stress patterns.

Murder in the Cathedral, then, is in many ways consistent with the remainder of Eliot's work. While it is not the only play he has written, it is by far the best in the sense that it contains the best poetry and the most coherent drama. The other plays will be reviewed briefly, but none of them warrant as full a study as *Murder in the Cathedral.* Again, Eliot's major contribution is not in the realm of verse drama, and the importance of the plays lies not in themselves but rather in what they led to. But it would be unfair to dismiss Eliot's dramatic work as utterly insignificant in itself. He made possible a renewed interest in verse drama in the twentieth century by offering poets a verse form compatible with the new accents of modern speech and capable of containing the ideas and the actions of a new society, quite different from the one Shakespeare wrote for at the height of the only other major period in the writing of verse drama.

BRIEF NOTES ON OTHER PLAYS

The play *Murder in the Cathedral* is generally considered Eliot's best play, and as a result it is the one most commonly studied. Eliot has of course written a number of other plays. This section will take up some of them. In no sense should these be considered "minor" works. Eliot's plays are, in a sense, his largest coherent works. They are statements of the problems he has discussed before, and they contain the same kinds of solutions to those problems that have appeared in the poetry. In general, one may say that the plays parallel the poetry quite closely. The two fragments which make up the incomplete *Sweeney Agonistes* attempt to handle dramatically the ideas of *The Waste Land.* It has already been pointed out that *Murder in the Cathedral* bears a strong similarity to *Ash Wednesday. The Family Reunion,* unlike the others, anticipates rather than follows the poem it most resembles. Coming between *Burnt Norton* and the remaining *Quartets,* it attempts to present dramatically the discovery which is their subject.

THE FAMILY REUNION

Like *Murder in the Cathedral, The Family Reunion* (1939) employs the chorus of classic Greek drama, but in this instance the chorus is made up of aunts and uncles, reminiscent of the chorus in Gilbert and Sullivan's *H. M. S. Pinafore,* rather than the chorus representing the people, as in *Murder in the Cathedral.* The play is characterized by a flatness in the conversation, contrasting with the richness of the dialogue in *Murder.* The verse, however, is quite remarkable in terms of the metrical experimentation noted earlier in these Notes. In comparison with *Murder,* the intensity of the drama is quite relaxed. The play suffers, perhaps, from too great subtlety for oral presentation. The themes of the need for the expiation of sin and of the evils of the family and of society, the latter reminiscent of *The Waste Land,* are employed in this play as they are in much of the poetry The play is a tragicomic verse melodrama.

The plot of *The Family Reunion* is quite weak. It owes a debt to *The Oresteia* by Aeschylus. Briefly, for Amy's birthday, in March—a month heralding the spring—the family assemble at Wishwood, Amy's house in the north of England. Again, there is little overt action, since the plot is psychological. Harry, the protagonist, absent for eight years, is coming to the reunion. A year ago Harry's wife mysteriously disappeared from an ocean liner. Harry arrives, behaving strangely, and shortly gives evidence that he is pursued by the Furies, the Eumenides. The family engage in some fairly civil conversation, all at cross purposes and all trivial, and then Harry announces, quite casually, that he murdered his wife. The remainder of the play is concerned with Harry's movement toward an understanding which will make possible expiation of his crime. The philosophical implications of the play are extremely complex.

In *The Waste Land,* Eliot demonstrated the thesis that suffering means purgation of sin. The suffering demands endurance of hell. In *Murder in the Cathedral,* Eliot carried the idea further, positing that suffering and action are identical; that is, to suffer or endure is to live, and to live is, inevitably, to act. As Thomas indicates, all who act rightly are martyrs. This, in a less apparent way, is also the theme of *The Family Reunion.*

This play demonstrates two worlds, like *Murder in the Cathedral.* The "normal" world, illustrated by the knights in the earlier play, contains a group of shallow, selfish people: Amy, Violet, Ivy, Gerald, and Charles. John and Arthur, who do not actually appear in the play, are also included in this category. The second, or "spiritual" world is represented only by Agatha, equivalent of Dante's Beatrice. Harry, the protagonist, is between these two worlds. At the beginning of the play, Harry is a kind of Gerontion, identifying himself with the past. As the play progresses, he comes to see first, that he is the victim of a kind of family curse, that he is a son of Adam, excluded from Eden not for any fault of his own, but for a sin committed by his ancestors. He learns that within the insane hell of spiritual despair there exists a potential state of reconciliation, and that the means for the attainment of that reconciliation is suffering. During the course of the play, Agatha commissions Harry to seek release from the wheel, not by denying the past, but by recognizing that "everything is irrevocable" and that "the future can only be built/ Upon the real past." Finally, Harry turns away from Agatha, renouncing spiritual values of human relationship as he has earlier renounced sexual ones in the murder of his wife. He goes in search of spiritual values symbolized by God as "the single eye above the desert" (see the Great Seal of the United States on the back of any one dollar bill). Like the Hollow Men, he rejects eyes to seek eyes. He leaves to atone through suffering, either by suffering or by action and in so doing he turns away from the things of the senses, severing himself wholly from the love of created beings to seek the love of God. He crosses from the "dream kingdom" of the Hollow Men into "death's twilight kingdom." Now, by performing a ritual self-sacrifice, as the family's Issac, Harry can celebrate the true birthday and the true family reunion.

Additional complications are added to the already complex situation, because Harry's understanding of his problem occurs on the psychological rather than on the theological level, and further because other elements in the plot add greater involution. Vengefulness and love between Amy and Agatha form a subplot working frictionally under the base plot, for example. The complex consideration of time as an element in the problem, with Amy serving as an exponent of mathematical time and Harry as an exponent of Bergsonian Duree as filtered through T. E. Hulme, adds still another layer of complexity.

As has been noted, the play was not a tremendous success, because no audience merely listening to a play can be expected to follow so complex a maze, particularly when the keys to the complexity are hidden in literary allusion which in turn is concealed in the dialogue.

THE COCKTAIL PARTY

The Cocktail Party (1949) is a versified drawing room comedy with a theme of serious spiritual quest. Like The Family Reunion, it is heavily indebted to the tradition of ritual drama. This play is more successful than The Family Reunion because it takes into account the difficulties of an audience trying to understand the oral presentation.

The plot, concerning domestic relations, is fairly clear. It concerns a series of "triangles." Edward Chamberlayne, a lawyer, is estranged from his wife, Lavinia. She, in turn, is in love with a young screen writer named Peter Quilpe who is in love with Celia Coplestone, a poetess, but Celia is Edward's mistress and is in love with him. Lavinia is not loved by anyone, and Edward loves no one. The play opens in the Chamberlayne London apartment where everyone except Lavinia is attending a cocktail party. She has just left Edward, and he, using the story that she is visiting a sick aunt, is playing solitary host to his guests. There are three other guests at the party; Julia Shuttlethwiate, an impertinent gossip, Alexander Mac-Colgie Gibbs, a world traveler somehow connected with the British Foreign Office, and a stranger unknown to Edward who later turns out to be Sir Henry Harcourt-Reilly, a psychologist. Act I is devoted to the exposition of the break between Edward and Celia and to the return of Lavinia. In scene i, Edward is questioned by Sir Henry, who promises that Lavinia will return. Later he hears Peter confess his love for Celia. In scene ii Celia separates from Edward, and in scene iii, on the next afternoon, Edward is again visited by Sir Henry. Lavinia returns, and she and Edward pick up their lives where they left them — in disagreement. Act II, several weeks later, takes place in Sir Henry's office. It turns out that Lavinia's return has been the result of a conspiracy arranged by Sir Henry to reconcile the Chamberlaynes. Sir Henry, who has been treating Lavinia, convinces them to try again to live together. Later, Sir Henry has an interview with Celia in which he encourages her to order her life. The choice she makes, although she does not perceive it, constitutes a life of potential sainthood or martyrdom. In Act III, several years later, another cocktail party is about to begin. The Chamberlaynes, now living happily together, are again the hosts. The characters all drop in accidentally, except Celia. Sir Henry tells the group that Celia had joined a medical missionary group and had gone out to a remote outpost in a country called Kinkanja. During an epidemic, the heathen inhabitants rebelled against the christianized ones, and Celia was crucified. Sir Henry reveals that he foresaw her violent death. The remainder of the act disperses the visitors and leaves the Chamberlaynes alone, waiting for the cocktail party to begin.

Sir Henry is the central figure in the play, at least until he reveals his identity in Act II. He has a certain authority over the other characters. That authority is not absolute, since no one is forced to obey him and since he does not dictate their choices. But, nothing can happen in the play until he acts. He has greater wisdom than any of the characters, and he has a clairvoyant faculty. Since the unfolding of the plot depends on what Sir Henry does, and since the characters respond only to what he does, the relationship between Sir Henry and the characters resembles the relationship between God and man. Furthermore, underlying the apparent structure of the play is a substructure based upon ritual atonement.

The play, as Eliot has said, is based on the *Alcestis* of Euripides. Sir Henry has his roots in the tradition of the "wise-Fool." Eliot, in "The Beating of a Drum"(1923) did a study of the ritual origins of the fools in Shakespeare's plays. His study demonstrates that the wise but unheeded advisor derives from the medicine man. Sir Henry is presented as a wise-fool. His two cohorts, Julia and Alex, together with him, are designated "the Guardians," constituting a kind of trilogy affecting the activities of mortals. The other characters are carefully juxtaposed in opposite pairs. Edward and Lavinia are similar in their dispassionate conservatism, but are contrasted with Celia and Peter who are imaginative and rebellious. But simultaneously, Edward and Lavinia are contrasted, as their incompatability clearly demonstrates, while Celia is able to achieve patience, and ultimately a greater fate, than Peter. All of these characters, except Peter, are enabled in the course of the play, to abnegate their wills to a greater cause. Peter is left, at the end of the play with the possibility of maturing. Sir Henry says of him: "He has not yet come to where the words are valid." The *yet* implies that he well may. In short, Eliot depicts human relationships which are in themselves totally unsatisfactory. Those who think they are in love are unable to marry, while those who are married are not in love but merely endure with each other. Each learns something in the course of the unfolding of the plot. Edward, at first a Gerontion figure, learns that sex and love are not identical and that time is irreversible. Celia, because she has greater potential, goes further; she learns that one can be liberated into a timelessness, an absorptive love.

Again, the play has connections in other of Eliot's works. Celia's sacrifice has mystical meaning in terms of the path suggested by St. John of the Cross and already explored by Eliot in *Ash Wednesday*. Edward, as has already been noted, is at least at first, a Gerontion. The ideas of the personal quest for atonement through suffering and action have been thoroughly explored in a number of earlier works.

The play is more actable than *The Family Reunion,* but it lacks the dramatic impact of *Murder in the Cathedral*. In some ways, its success derives from the fact that it is a burlesque of Eliot's own poetic symbols. Certainly its success derives from the fact that Eliot recognized the difficulty of the audience in comprehending what he was doing. In attempting to clarify his plot, however, he had to sacrifice his verse.

THE CONFIDENTIAL CLERK

This play (1953) is a farce, based on the *Ion* of Euripides. It is a strange play for Eliot, since it contains no saints and no geniuses. The theme of the play may be stated as: "A free approach to the meaning of one's life can redeem and remake the past." The plot concerns the unravelling of the identity of a bastard.

The play is set within the London household of Sir Claude Mulhammer. Sir Claude's confidential secretary, Eggerson, is about to retire and he is going to be replaced by Colby Simpkins. Lady Elizabeth, Sir Claude's wife, is returning from abroad, and Sir Claude wants Eggerson to prepare her for the new secretary. Eggerson is to tell her that he is retiring for reasons of health, but the truth is that Sir Claude believes Colby to be his bastard son. Lady Elizabeth is a confused woman, addicted to religious and philosophical fads. The household also contains a girl named Lucasta Angel, illegitimate daughter of Sir Claude. The Mulhammers have no children of their own, although Lady Elizabeth had an illegitimate son who seems to have disappeared. A Mrs. Guzzard is brought in later to clear up the problems, for she, like Little Buttercup in *H. M. S. Pinafore,* apparently had practiced baby farming.

The plot, as it unfolds, explores the problem of human sympathy to an extent never previously approached by Eliot. It also explores the problem of reality in a somewhat different sense than Eliot has previously used it. Sir Claude has become a financier to expiate his own sin of having resisted his father's advice. His real inclination was to be an artist. He has adjusted to the facts of necessity, and he has set aside a room in his house for his activities as an artistic potter. That room constitutes his "real" world, while the business of finance is merely an avocation. The substitute life, says Sir Claude, "...begins as a kind of make-believe/ And the make-believing makes it real." But it becomes apparent that the dream world of art into which Sir Claude retires is also a make believe world. Thus, he lives in two worlds, both of which are unreal. In this sense he is like his wife who also lives in worlds of make-believe. Colby is faced with a similar decision, for he wants to be an artist, not a financier like Sir Claude, but he feels the obligation of his paternity.

As the plot develops, however, it turns out, in a very complex scene at the end of the play that Colby is not Sir Claude's son, but the legitimate son of the Guzzards, and that a character known as B. Kaghan, Lucasta's boyfriend, is actually Lady Elizabeth's long lost illegitimate son. Colby then, is free to cultivate his own garden.

The poetry of the play is very weak. The lines spoken by the characters are printed in a verse typography, but they are really a kind of prose, and they are dominated by a prose cadence. There are practically no symbolic objects in the play, and the only symbolic reference is to Eggerson's garden. But, the characterization is the best of any of Eliot's plays. There is no wise fool in this play, and there is no central character around whom all the others revolve. Rather, in this play, each character makes his own diagnosis of his problem and provides his own prescription for a solution. The play has only tenuous connections with Eliot's other work. Colby Simpkins has some relationship to Celia Coplestone of *The Cocktail Party* in the sense that he too has a spiritual hunger, but he makes no sacrifice comparable to hers. He does, it is suggested at the end of the play, find a life regulated harmoniously through understanding. Eggerson serves as a model for his aim. The play affirms freedom of choice. Like *The Family Reunion,* this play suggests that a free approach to the meaning of one's life can redeem and remake the past.

A GENERAL EVALUATION

The work of a poet like T. S. Eliot is difficult to evaluate generally. Perhaps the best evaluation of his total impact came from a man who did not believe in what he was doing. William Carlos Williams, writing in *I Wanted to Write a Poem* (1958), has this to say about T. S. Eliot:

> I had a violent feeling that Eliot had betrayed what I believed in. He was looking backward; I was looking forward. He was a conformist, with wit, learning that I did not possess... But I felt that he had rejected America and I refused to be rejected... I realized the responsibility I must accept. I knew he would influence all subsequent American poets and take them out of my sphere. ...It was shocking to me that he was so tremendously successful.

There is no question that Eliot has been successful. His poetry lends itself to explication, as the countless books explicating his poetry exemplify. His poetry has characteristics which appeal to the classroom teacher, and he has been given to high school or college students since his work became broadly accepted at about the time of the second World War. No young poet writing today can have entirely escaped the influence of Eliot if he is writing within the limitations of the Anglo-American tradition. This is neither necessarily all good nor all bad. Certainly Eliot has made a significant contribution to modern literature. His work with time, with the interweaving of levels of symbolic meaning, his exploration of certain archetypal myth patterns, his juxtaposition of past and present to make the past more meaningful in the present, his insistence that the past is irredeemable and irrevocable, all of these constitute important philosophical contributions. His explorations in rhythm and poetic structure which have resulted in a new poetic idiom capable of including the rhythms of modern speech and suitable to the structure of modern ideas also constitutes a serious, in fact a profound, contribution. But there is something inherently unhealthy in the fact that a single poet has been able to dominate the creative stage for so long a time.

There is no question that young poets will be able to build upon the foundation which he created. But Eliot himself has stressed the freedom of the will. This is not to say that Eliot is consciously imposing his will on his followers, but rather that his disciples will impose their wills, which are interpretations of his will, and that thereby they will create a generation of poets who are not indebted to Eliot, but who are, rather, poor carbon copies of him.

The greatest danger lies in the fact that Eliot's poetry is not a popular poetry. The recent history of literature has shown that poetry is constantly retreating farther and farther from the popular imagination. Eliot's poetry is too subtle in its effects and too complex in its philosophy to be a popular poetry. Those who follow him, perhaps unduly influenced by him, may help to move poetry still farther away from the popular imagination. That might be a tragedy in terms of the future of the language and its literature.

QUESTIONS

1. It has been pointed out several times that Eliot is very much indebted to Dante. Compare Eliot's view of the waste land with Dante's hell. Compare Eliot's view with Virgil's view of hell in the *Aeneid.*

2. What is the function of the tarot cards and what bearing does it have on the thematic structure of *The Waste Land?*

3. Many of Eliot's poems have epigrams preceding the text. In general, discuss Eliot's use of epigrams. What is the value of these quotations? Do they contribute anything to the poem? Would the poem be better or worse, easier or harder, without these references?

4. Compare *"The Love Song of J. Alfred Prufrock"* with Edward Arlington Robinson's poem *"Miniver Cheevy."*

5. Compare *"The Hollow Men"* with Robert Browning's poem *"Fra Lippo Lippi."*

6. Besides Eliot and Browning, many poets have employed the device of the dramatic monologue. What verse form has been most commonly employed? Make a list of American poets who have written important dramatic monologues since 1900.

7. Compare *"The Journey of the Magi"* with William Butler Yeat's poem *"The Second Coming."*

8. Eliot's life has covered the period of the two World Wars, yet his poetry seems not to have been touched by the wars. How do you explain this fact?

9. Ezra Pound and T. S. Eliot have often been linked. Compare the technique employed by Pound in *"Canto I"* with Eliot's *"Gerontion."*

10. The second law of thermodynamics states that the universe tends to run down into chaos. The human mind, therefore, is an island of order in this sea of chaos. Does this theory have any bearing on Eliot's *Ash Wednesday?*

11. F. R. Leavis, writing about *The Waste Land,* says, "The unity the poem aims at is that of an inclusive consciousness." In so far as you can, tell what he means. Does that statement appear to be true or false? Why?

12. In 1919, in an essay entitled "Hamlet and His Problems," Eliot propounded the idea of something he called the "Objective Correlative." He wrote:

> An artist must find an Objective Correlative; that is, a set of objects, a situation, a chain of events which shall be the formula of that particular emotion, and which will then evoke that emotion in the reader.

The theory rests on the assumption that the poet is trying to express an emotion, and not on the assumption that he is trying to understand that emotion. To what extent does the idea of the Objective Correlative seem to apply in *The Waste Land?* How is it worked out?

13. Alfred Tennyson wrote a verse drama called *Becket,* also based on the life of Thomas à Becket, Archbishop of Canterbury. Compare Tennyson's text with Eliot's. Which is the more dramatic? Which contains the better poetry? Which is more historically accurate?

14. *The Cocktail Party* has been defined as a versified drawing-room comedy. Compare it with any play by Noel Coward.

15. Compare the biographical verse drama *Murder in the Cathedral* (1935) with Maxwell Anderson's biographical verse drama *Elizabeth the Queen* (1930).

16. Both the United States and England claim T. S. Eliot. In your opinion, is he a British poet or an American poet? Justify your decision on internal evidence drawn from the poetry, NOT on biographical data.

17. In *The Waste Land,* as in several other poems, Eliot has drawn on his knowledge of Eastern religion. Is it valid for a poet to draw on esoteric knowledge, or does such material tend to defeat any attempt at communication with his reader?

18. In general, does Eliot communicate with his reader, or is his poetry so *intentionally* obscure and personal that no communication is possible? Justify your answer by specific reference to particular poems or parts of them.

19. Eliot has also written something called *Old Possum's Book of Practical Cats.* In what way is the verse in this book consistent or inconsistent with the usual content of Eliot's poetry?

20. Is there any humor at all in Eliot's poetry, or is everything completely serious. In your answer, refer specifically to *The Waste Land* and any other single work.

21. *The Confidential Clerk* has been called a farce. Compare it with John Gay's *Beggar's Opera* (1728).

22. There is an apocryphal story that a visitor to Eliot's home found a copy of Jessie Weston's book *From Ritual to Romance* unopened and uncut on Eliot's bookshelf. To what extent was Miss Weston's work *essential* to the writing of *The Waste Land*?

23. To what extent are the ideas of the Grail legend used in poems other than *The Waste Land*?

24. A great deal has been said in the Notes about Eliot's use of time in his poetry. To what extent is his use of time different from that of any other writer of dramatic monologue? From any writer of novels?

25. To what extent does Eliot's view of the earth as a kind of hell result from the social, economic, and political events of the first quarter of the twentieth century?

26. Is any particular political philosophy reflected in Eliot's verse? Is he a communist? A socialist? A democrat? A fascist?

27. Eliot has been accused of anti-semitism in connection with such poems as *Gerontion, The Waste Land, Burbank with a Baedeker,* and others. Do you find any justification for the change? Give specific evidence for your assertion from particular poems.

28. It has been pointed out that there are six published versions of *Murder in the Cathedral.* Compare any two of these versions. What changes has Eliot made? Is it possible to speculate about the reasons for those changes?

29. F. O. Matthiessen, in an article entitled "The System of Allusion," maintains that Eliot's notes to *The Waste Land* are superfluous and even misleading. Is he right? Why did Eliot add these notes? What purpose do they serve? Are they necessary? Do they tend to confuse the reader?

30. Perform your own careful analysis, following the method employed above in the Notes on *"The Lovesong of J. Alfred Prufrock"* and *The Waste Land,* on any one of the following poems:
     Portrait of a Lady
     The Hippopotamus
     Whispers of Immortality
     La Figlia Che Piange
     Mr. Eliot's Sunday Morning Service
     Sweeney Among the Nightingales
How does such an analysis help you to understand the poem better? Does it help at all, or can you *appreciate* the poem without *understanding* it?

NOTES

NOTES

NOTES

NOTES

NOTES

NOTES